The Keys to Creation

Consciously Create All You Desire!

Michelle Orlijan

DEDICATION

I'm dedicating this book to my spirit guides, who have helped me to thoroughly understand and utilize this information for my own benefit, as well as offering the assistance to be able to share it with others.

CONTENTS

INTRODUCTION

Everything is energy! That is the beginning of every workshop that I have taught. Whether it was a class in Mastering Manifestation, Energy Healing, Chakra Clearing and Balancing, Communicating with Spirit, Tarot Reading, Crystals, or Past Lives, it is all based on energy, which is "All That Is".

Once there is a realization of this, then we can go deeper into what our reality truly is, because it isn't what most people think it is. In this book, we will take a closer look at energy and how that relates to our physical experience and what we believe to be our "reality". Things that seem very fixed and "real", such as time, space, and our physical experience, are much more fluid than most people realize.

There are also Universal Laws that are part of our experience. Just like gravity is a law of physics that we experience on this planet, there are other laws that are just as consistent for both the physical world and the higher vibrational dimensions. With an understanding of what these laws are and how they work, you can use them as tools to create the "reality" that you desire. What is called "magic" by some is just utilizing the unseen forces of energy to manifest a desired outcome. We are creating our realities, whether we realize it or not, but to do so consciously will create a much more desirable outcome.

As important it is to understand how the Universe works, it is equally important, if not more so, to understand ourselves and the energy that is flowing through our bodies. That is the key to everything. Most people are blocking the flow of energy through their body, and that creates resistance and affects the ability to create in a positive way. It is thoughts, emotions, and beliefs that create these energetic blockages. So there needs to be some self-introspection to determine if your energetic vibration is as high as it can be. Your emotions, health, and overall state of wellbeing will be an indicator, but there are other ways to check this as well. If energy is flowing freely, you will feel happy, healthy, and you will be attracting the things you desire into your experience.

This book will be separated into three sections. The first will be about energy, how the Universe works, and who you are as a multi-dimensional being. The second section will be about how to develop an awareness of your personal energy flow and vibration, and it will provide the tips and tools to improve it from any level that you are currently at. The third section will be discussing in detail exactly how to create everything you desire in life. Each section is vitally important to a complete understanding and implementation of the steps involved in creating everything you desire.

This book will combine scientific information, along with ancient knowledge, and practical tools for implementation. Everything will be expressed as clearly as possible. If you follow the steps and guidelines as they are presented, you will create everything in life you desire. This is just how the Universe works, and once you have the knowledge and implement it, you will see for yourself. You will then be an example for others. The higher dimensional part of yourself knows your true power, now it is time for you to recognize it as well.

Key #1:
Understanding How the
Universe Works

THE STRUCTURE OF EXISTENCE

There are basic principles that apply to the structure of existence. These are laws of nature that apply to every aspect of the Universe, at all dimensional levels, both the physical world and higher vibrational realities. With an understanding of how the Universe works, you can utilize that knowledge to your advantage in creating the reality you desire.

We will go through each of these in more detail within this section of the book, as well as other important information to understand about who you are and how the Universe works.

These are the key principles that apply to all of existence. You may find others expressing these in different ways or adding other laws, but they are all based from these same principles.

1) "All That Is" is Vibration and Consciousness.

Everything is energy! It has movement and it is mental. This describes the structure of the Universe at all vibrational and dimensional levels.

2) The Law of Divine Oneness

Everything and everyone are part of and are connected through the Universal energy field of All That Is.

3) Everything is Here and Now

Time and space are an illusion. "All That Is" exists without the limitations of time and space. There is only here and now.

4) The Law of Attraction

What you send out, is what you receive back. Since everything is vibration, you receive back what is a match to the vibration that you are and that you are sending out through your thoughts and emotions. Everything you experience is only a reflection of consciousness.

5) The Principle of Polarity

There are two sides to everything and a balance between them. Hot and cold, high and low, happy and sad, or masculine and feminine are examples. Opposites are the same thing and are identical in nature, but they vary in degrees or vibration. Hot and cold are both temperature, but they are different degrees of the same thing. Because they are the same, you cannot have one without the other. You have an awareness of one because of the contrast of the other. You wouldn't understand happiness, if sadness did not exist. Everything exists on a sliding scale of vibration.

6) The Law of Cause and Effect

There is a reason for absolutely everything. Every cause has an effect, and every effect has a cause. Nothing is random. Every thought, emotion, and action are creating your experience. This includes what was set in motion from your higher dimensional consciousness before you incarnated in this life.

7) The Principle of Rhythm

Everything changes and moves in cycles. There is always a movement towards balance. A pendulum that swings in one direction will return to the other. We experience these cycles in day and night, birth and death, the seasons of the planet. You are never stuck in the same place, as there is always potential for change.

8) Harmony in All

Nothing in the Universe is random or done in chaos. There is a harmony to nature. There are rhythms and patterns that hold everything together through a divine symmetry.

EVERYTHING IS ENERGY!

Everything in the Universe is energy. That energy is just vibrating at different rates of speed. Whether we are looking at a subatomic particle or a chair, they are all the same thing. Physical matter is a vibrating much slower, so it appears dense, but it is really made of the same subatomic particles that are part of "All That Is". The same energy that is not limited by time and space. This is the energy that we are all a part of, and it is what connects us all.

So, what is this energy? This field that everything is comprised of has consciousness and force. It is the combination that creates worlds and everything that exists within them. Our souls, the higher dimensional part of ourselves, because they are not limited by space and time, can experience a deeper sense of connection to this unified field of energy. We are created from and are connected to this source energy, or what some would call "God". Because our physical bodies are vibrating at a lower speed than the higher dimensional part of ourselves, we don't feel as connected to the Universal consciousness of "All That

Is". Despite the experience, the separation we feel is only an illusion.

Our bodies are just a temporary vehicle we use to create, experience, and grow. The part of our soul that comes into the physical body is just a very small part of who we really are. The larger part of us remains in non-physical form. We are able to connect with that higher dimensional part of ourselves, but because most people don't realize who they really are, and they think of themselves as what they are experiencing in this physical reality, most people are not aware of the connection to their true self.

This disconnection causes resistance and blocks the flow of energy, which affects everything. Your energetic vibration affects your overall wellbeing in all areas mentally, emotionally, spiritually, as well as your physical health. It also affects your ability to manifest everything you desire.

At the higher dimensional, non-physical levels of energy, there are not the same limitations that we have in the physical world. Even though our physical bodies and the world and everything in it are the same energy, our bodies and everything in the physical world are vibrating at a much slower rate, and therefore we have the experience of being limited by space, time, and a lack of connection to our true selves.

People tend to identify themselves based on their experience in their physical reality. They think of themselves as who they are by their gender, race, religion, politics, what they do for a career, social status, and by what role they play in their families. All of those things are just temporary and have nothing to do with who you truly are at a soul level, which is your true self. This life is a very temporary experience, and if we view ourselves solely on this experience, we lose the true power in who we really are.

We are multi-dimensional beings, and even though we are living in a 3D reality, we can utilize the higher dimensional energies along with a blend of both science and ancient knowledge to consciously create our reality. We can also use this information and energy to heal our bodies and maintain physical health, slow down the aging process, and to maintain a sense of peace and balance in any situation.

The truth is that you are an eternal being of light, a non-physical consciousness, that has chosen to experience what you are creating in this physical reality.

We are all one. We are part of the Divine Oneness of the collective consciousness, which is the universal living mind. We are created from and connected to Source Energy. If we can see beyond the illusion of our experience in the physical realm, we can tap into the energy of the creative source.

We are part of the energy that creates worlds. We have that same power. We are connected to all of the knowledge that exists in the Universe. We don't have to be limited to what we are experiencing in this physical body.

HOW REAL IS OUR "REALITY"?

Our physical "reality" is not quite as "real" as it seems. When we look at energy at the smallest level, the subatomic level, the energy that exists between the atom nucleus and the electron, we start to see some aspects of energy that are determined by consciousness and are not limited by space or time.

Atoms are the building blocks of absolutely everything in the physical universe. They are made of a nucleus that includes neutrons and protons that are surrounded by one or more electrons. The space between the nucleus and electrons appears to be empty space, but it is actually part of a field of energetic frequencies that are completely interconnected throughout the Universe.

Science has proven that the subatomic particles within this connected energy field that is "All That Is", react to consciousness. The electrons exist simultaneously in an infinite number of possibilities, until the observer focuses their attention or awareness on them. Then that part of the invisible field of energy and information becomes a particle in the physical world. Once the observer takes their mind off of it, it changes back into a wave of energy and is no longer observable. It still exists as potential in the field of creation. That particle of physical matter doesn't appear to exist until we observe it. The moment we are no longer putting our attention on it, it turns back into energy and into possibility. This shows that our consciousness has an effect on energy and matter.

We are living what is basically a virtual reality projection. The higher dimensional part of ourselves is guiding us on this journey that is created by our consciousness, through our thoughts and emotions. We experience this as being "real", but it is only an experience of what we are projecting with our consciousness from an energetic field, where all potentials exist here and now and are "real".

Most people think of their consciousness as being within the body, but it is actually the body that is within consciousness. The brain is only a receiver and transmitter of energy. It allows for the experience of physical reality. It receives energetic information and translates it into what we can perceive through our physical senses.

What we experience through our physical senses of sight, sound, smell, touch, and taste is how we perceive our physical reality. The role of the brain is to process these energetic signals from various sense organs and give them meaning. Other beings we share this planet with perceive physical reality differently than we do. Some animals see light and color and hear sounds that have vibrations that are outside of human perception. As an example, dogs have a much greater sense of hearing and smell than we do, have better night vision, but don't see nearly as many colors as we do. We could be experiencing at the same things and perceive them very differently. Other animals have senses that can detect forms of energy that are invisible to us, such as magnetic and electrical fields. How we perceive our physical reality is dependent on our specific sensory organs, and what ranges of vibration that we can detect, as well as our brains ability to process that energetic information. Imagine what we could perceive if we were not limited by our physical bodies.

Time is not what it seems to be either. We experience time moving in a line, with a past, present, and future. However, this is only how we experience time in our physical reality. This allows us the ability to experience what we are creating in a linear form, but that is only our perspective, because time is actually fluid. What we experience as time is an illusion that is based on our perception.

Einstein's general theory of relativity established time as a physical thing. It is part of space-time, created by the gravitational field produced by massive objects, such as our planet. Time is not an absolute. Every object in the Universe has its own time running at a pace determined by the local gravitational field. Speed affects time as well, with a rate of time reaching zero as it approaches the speed of light. Therefore, the massless particles that are the energetic field of "All That Is" that travel at or above the speed of light are unaffected by the passage of time.

We also can take in to account the possibility of what we experience is a result of the human brain and mentality. Time is a reflection of change, what we are tapping into moment by moment by moment, and our brains may construct a sense of time as if it were flowing. Think of a roll of film at a movie theater. All of the frames on the film exist all at once, but the projector light shining through them one at a time, gives the experience of it moving from one part of the movie to the next. Think of your consciousness as that projector light.

At higher dimensions, time doesn't exist in the way we experience from our perspective. In the higher dimensional reality there is only the "now". There is only one moment in creation. Everything exists at the same time in the field of potentials. We are experiencing it from different points of view, because of our perspective of time that we experience in physical reality. We experience what we are tapping into with our consciousness moment by moment, but that is only the way it appears based on our perception of time. From a non-physical perspective that is not limited by the illusion of space and time, nothing changes. Everything exists here and now. It is only our perspective and point of view that changes from our self-imposed limitations of the physical world, and therefore our experiences change.

Einstein is quoted as saying "The only reason for time is so that everything doesn't happen at once." "Time and space are modes by which we think and not conditions in which we live." "The distinction between the past, present and future is only a stubbornly persistent illusion."

With quantum entanglement, multiple particles are linked together in such a way that the measurement of one particle's quantum state determines the states of the other particles. This connection is not dependent on the location of the particles in space. If you separate entangled particles by billions of miles, changing one particle through consciousness, it will induce a change in the others instantaneously. This is not due to information being sent to the location of other particles through the field, it is because the energy field of "All That Is" is holographic in nature, and every part contains the whole. Since absolutely everything in the Universe is comprised of these subatomic particles, nothing is separate from anything else. It is all an illusion.

In quantum events, consciousness plays a part in what happens, and they are not affected by the passage of time or the location in space. Both time and space both cease to exist entirely.

If time and space don't truly exist in the way we think that they do and what we perceive is limited by our senses and brain, is anything "real", or is it just what we have created to experience as "real" from a higher dimensional non-physical state? Another Albert Einstein quote is "Reality is merely an illusion, albeit a very persistent one."

It is only the experience that is "real", and we create the experience with our consciousness.

WHO ARE YOU?

We now know that most of us are not exactly who we think of ourselves as, so who are you? You are an eternal multi-dimensional being of light that is a part of The Creative Source, or what some would call God, or All That Is.

If you can see the bigger picture of who you are, and get beyond thinking of yourself based off of your experiences and labels that you created in this physical experience, you will realize that you are so much more. You have the ability to utilize the power that creates worlds, as it is a part of you. You came here to create your experience.

At a soul level, the closest adjective that would describe your true self and All That Is would be unconditional love. It is more than that, but as far as our understanding, that would be the closest way to describe who you truly are.

The energy of your higher self is non-physical. It doesn't have the denseness of physical matter. It is not limited by space and time that we experience in our physical bodies. It is a part of the divine oneness of All That Is. It is connected to unlimited knowledge and has an awareness of all potentials, as well as our life purpose or what we came into this physical realm to create for ourselves and others.

Now most people don't necessarily identify themselves as either love or as God, and that is because of not being aligned with their true selves. That separation we create from our true selves comes from identifying ourselves with our Ego or who we have created ourselves to be in this physical experience. Who we have created ourselves to be in this lifetime is based on our beliefs, thoughts, emotions, and behavior. We think we are who we are, but we are looking from a very limited perspective, and even the aspects that create who we experience ourselves to be in this physical reality are in our control to change.

The lack of alignment to our higher selves causes energetic blockages, and from that causes all kinds of problems in the areas of emotional and mental wellbeing and is also the cause of all physical health problems.

If you can clear your mind of all thought, let go of focus of any problems that you see in your "reality", let go of any of the labels you have identified yourself as based on this physical experience, and just be present in this moment, connect to your soul, and just be, all that is left is a feeling of love, and that is who you are.

In daily life, it is easy to get distracted with things we have to do with work, bills, laundry, figuring out what to eat for dinner, etc., but it is important to know who you truly are, and to know the power that you hold in creating the experience of this physical life.

Most people are aware of the idea of reincarnation and believe that there is something more than this life we are currently living. However, despite that, most people still tend to get caught up in what they are experiencing in this lifetime and think of the "costume" or "meat suit" they are wearing as who they are.

This would be like getting into your car and identifying yourself as that vehicle. If you are driving a grey SUV, you would identify yourself as fairly big, average, your color does not stand out, and you would be feeling every scratch or ding, as if every imperfection is a part of who you are. Obviously when you get into your car, you do not identify yourself as the car. However, most people tend to identify themselves with their bodies, which are also just vehicles.

In reality, your soul is who you are, and your body and mind are just what you temporarily use to create and experience from a different perspective.

Remember, the larger part of ourselves is still in non-physical form. We have a tendency to think of our soul or consciousness as being within our physical body, but really it is the physical body that is within our consciousness.

We are a higher dimensional energy. Part of that higher vibrational consciousness is guiding us through our intuition and emotion, which affects our thoughts, which then influences our actions, which together create our experience in our physical bodies. It is very similar to virtual reality, in which our higher mind is connecting to our physical selves to help guide this experience we call life.

Our higher selves communicate to us in our physical form through our intuition and emotion. From the information received through this way, then our brains can process the thoughts that tap into the field of potentials and create what we experience in life.

The problem with this is that most people do not listen to their intuition or what they receive at their heart mind, and solely focus on what they receive from the logical mind or brain, which is ruled by the Ego, or who they have created themselves to be in this physical reality. They may be drawn to something or have a sense of knowing, but if it doesn't make sense to the logical mind, most people will disregard it. The brain and therefore logical mind are only connected to the physical experience. Our higher mind, or soul, is connected to All That Is.

Also, the soul can guide through emotion as well. You have heard the saying to "follow your bliss". That is because that is your soul using that emotion of joy to guide you in the right direction.

When you are feeling lower vibrational emotions, such as sadness, anger, guilt, fear, anxiety, stress, resentment, etc., you are feeling those emotions because you are not aligned with your higher self, and those feelings are a guide to let you know that. Those feelings are created from your own thoughts and beliefs about what you are experiencing in life. Those lower vibrational emotions cause energetic blockages, that create resistance and block what you would ideally like to be experiencing. That energetic resistance can and will cause problems for you.

If you are in alignment with your higher self, then you feel more of a sense of who you really are. You feel joy, love, peace, and vitality. If you are not feeling like this, it is important to determine what thoughts or beliefs are causing the resistance and shift them. We will talk more about how to do that later in this book. Your emotions are an excellent indicator of your energetic vibration, and they will let you know if you are aligned with your higher self or not.

The higher your energetic vibration, or in other words the less resistance you have energetically, or the more aligned you are to your higher self, not only affects your overall wellbeing in all areas, but it also affects your ability to manifest what you desire to experience in life, and how quickly you can create what you want to experience.

If you are not feeling completely aligned with your higher self, that is ok, the entire second section of this book that will let you know how to remove the resistance and raise your energetic vibration. This is extremely important to master, because your energetic vibration affects everything you experience in your life.

We have all been here before, in many different bodies or "vehicles" or "costumes", to create and experience from many different perspectives. Not only have we had past lives on this planet, but many others as well. We have had many life experiences that were not human. At a soul level, we are part of Source energy that has no beginning or an end. We are eternal and have had many physical experiences way before the Earth was even created.

In spirit, in pure non-physical form, there is no space or time, everything in creation is instantaneous. The physical experience of life on Earth allows us to observe and experience the process of creation.

Our soul has those experiences from all of our lifetimes as well as being who we really are at a higher vibrational level. There is so much knowledge that we have acquired, and because we have a connection to that higher dimensional part of ourselves, we can connect to that information if we reduce the energetic resistance to allow it to flow through.

Many are aware of those people who seem to have natural gifts in different areas, whether it is music, art, sports, science, or anything else. Our higher self has all of the knowledge from what we have experienced as our past lives, and it can guide us to complete things we have started or enjoyed in past lives and lead us to that knowledge through our intuition.

We don't come into our physical reality alone either. We have soul groups or families that we choose to incarnate with. Those occasions where you feel a deep connection with someone you just met are because at a soul level you have a connection. Sometimes these soul connections are people who are very prominent in your current life, and sometimes they may just come in for a short time to help one of you with a lesson you wanted to learn or for a karmic debt from a past life experience. Sometimes you may just connect to have that continued relationship.

There is help from the higher dimensions as well. We have spiritual guides, higher dimensional energies from star families, and others we have known at that soul level that are available to help guide us on this journey of life as well. The key is to reduce resistance and raise your vibration, so you can more easily receive the guidance that is there for you.

We come into the physical realm to create and experience. Before we come in physically, we develop a plan of who we want to connect with, what we want to accomplish, to bring balance from past experiences, and sometimes it is an opportunity to react to a lesson from a past life in a different way through a different perspective.

An example of a karmic lesson or learning from a different perspective would be if you were in a past life as a wealthy powerful person that took advantage of someone less fortunate, in the next life you may come in as someone less fortunate that isn't being treated fairly. This is not about punishment. It is about bringing balance and experiencing something from a different perspective and learning and growing from it.

The life plan is developed through our soul consciousness, and therefore is energetically in the realm of all potentials for us to tap into with the assistance of our higher selves to guide us through our intuition.

The answer to the question of who you are is that you are an eternal multidimensional being of light, you are a part of God, The Creative Source, and the energetic field of consciousness that is All That Is.

At a soul level, while we have our individual consciousnesses and experiences, we are all part of the Divine Oneness, and we are all creating together.

THE FIELD OF ALL POTENTIALS

There is an energetic field of all potentials, that we have mentioned briefly in this book already. This energetic "reality" is just as real as our physical reality. Actually, it is more so, because our physical realities are just temporary and are not quite as "real" as they may seem. Again, just because we can't see it or feel it with the limited senses we have in the physical realm, doesn't mean it does not exist.

All possibilities of our physical reality exist as electromagnetic potentials in this quantum field. These possibilities exist as frequency or energy that is carrying information.

It is when our consciousness highlights a potential through our thoughts and we follow through with inspired action, then we will be able to experience it in our physical reality. Everything already exists and is tapped into first in this energetic field before we can experience it in our physical reality.

Our thoughts are higher dimensional energies. Because of this higher rate of vibration that is not limited by space and time, our consciousness can immediately tap into the energetic field of all potentials, and we can select the options that are most preferred by putting our focus and thoughts on those preferred options.

You just have to tune into the energy of what is already in the field through your thoughts, emotions, and intentions. The higher dimensional part of yourself will guide you through your intuition to direct you to the highest potentials that are already there energetically. You do need to listen to the intuition and take the inspired action needed to move you forward in order to bring the potential into your reality in the physical world.

Many people are unconsciously tapping into options that they may not prefer, and creating things they don't want, because that is where their attention and thoughts are. There is great power in mastering the mind by controlling our thoughts. Everything we experience is first crystalized energetically before it is experienced in our physical reality.

This field of all potentials available for your physical experience is constantly changing, as your thoughts, emotions, and actions are changing. As you tap into the field through your consciousness, you are creating your reality through your thoughts.

You have some potentials that are in the field that were highlighted there before you came into this material world in this incarnation. There are things that you decided you wanted to come here to accomplish and also karmic energies there as well, that create different circumstances, opportunities, or connections for you during this lifetime. I'm sure some of you are aware of soul mates, and connections between people that you know were destined to happen. This energetic information was consciously highlighted in the field before you came into this incarnation.

You may be familiar with the Rumi quote "what you seek is seeking you". That is because it is in the field already, and the higher dimensional part of yourself is guiding you through your intuition and emotion to bring it into your physical experience. You will be drawn to what you are a vibrational match to, and what is a vibrational match will also be attracted to you. It is similar to the force of two magnets being pulled together.

The potentials of past, present, and future all exist at the same time. There isn't the limitation of time or space in this field of energy. Everything is "now". There is only one moment in creation. We are experiencing it from different points of view, because of our perspective of time that we experience in physical reality. We experience what we are tapping into with our consciousness moment by moment, but that is only the way it appears based on our perception of time.

Again, think of the example of the roll of film at the movie theatre. As we use our consciousness through our thoughts to shine the light through what is already there (past, present, and future) in this energetic field of all potentials, we experience these events we are creating in a linear fashion. Because of how we focus our thoughts, moving from one moment to the next, that is how we experience the events we are creating. Also, the way our brains perceive time also allows for this experience of time moving from one moment to the next.

In higher dimensions, things can be created very quickly. There are other planets with higher vibrations, where it is very easy for beings to create what they desire, in some cases almost instantaneously. Because Earth is such a low vibration and very dense, it takes time for things to shift from the energetic reality to the physical one. It does happen, but it does take time, or what we experience as time here on Earth.

The higher your personal energetic vibration, the quicker you can experience what you are creating, but it may still require some patience. We chose to come into a lower vibrational reality, where the manifestation process is slower and more limited, so that we could observe and experience the process of creation and learn and grow from it.

It is easy to focus your thoughts and desires based on what you are currently experiencing in life, but remember that is old energy that created what you are currently experiencing. If you keep your thoughts there, then you are not creating what you want for the future. Don't focus your thoughts and attention to "what is" if it is not what you desire. It is better to focus your attention on what you would prefer to experience.

We can only "see" what is a vibrational match to ourselves. As we change our thoughts, ideas, and beliefs, then our vibration changes, and therefore what we see and experience changes.

The key is to be aware that you can tap into the potentials that you want to create by mastering your thoughts. Most people are just reacting to what they are experiencing, and they are allowing random thoughts and emotions to create their reality in chaos. You can consciously focus on that which you want to manifest, and if you have removed any energetic resistance, then it must become a part of your experience. That is how the Universe works.

If you can think it, it is in this energetic field as a potential to experience in your reality. Don't limit yourself by focusing your attention on things that you don't want in your life or by not thinking big enough to create new and wonderful things in your experience. You are a powerful creator, so use that power!

AS ABOVE, SO BELOW

You may have heard the saying "As Above, So Below". This has been used since ancient times. The "above" and "below" are not locations, they are higher and lower levels of energetic vibration.

This means we are the same as the creative source. We are a spark of that same energy that created universes and worlds. We are all creators, and that is what we came here to experience!

This phrase has another meaning as well. We are in the lower vibrational material world, and that is the physical reality that we experience. The energetic field of all potentials is a higher vibrational reality, that we will refer to as "the field".

Everything in the field is tapped into through consciousness. What you experience in physical reality is created through energy, in the form of thoughts and emotions, that crystalizes potentials of a matching vibration in the energetic field (as above). Once tapped into through your attention, those potentials of a matching vibration can then be made visible to you in your experience of physical reality (so below).

Everything you see and think of as reality is manifest consciousness. Your reality is a reflection of what you tapped into in the field through your thoughts and emotions, whether it was done intentionally or not. Your experience in your physical reality is a mirror of consciousness. Life itself is nothing more than energy that is vibrating at various frequencies. Think of your energy as a magnet that is attracting back what is a vibrational match.

We are all creating our reality, and there is power in knowing that you are in control, but that also means taking responsibility for what you did not consciously create as well. Taking responsibility doesn't mean blaming yourself. It means you know that you have the power to change anything that you are not currently happy with. Just change the way you are thinking, and you can change any situation.

Another meaning for this saying, "as above, so below", is that the universal laws apply not only to the 3D material world that we live in, but all dimensional realities. This includes the universal laws of creation.

SHIFTING REALITIES

As we are shifting through the field with our consciousness, our reality is constantly shifting. Remember, there is no past, present, and future in the field. There is only "now". Physical reality allows us to experience what already exists now from different points of view. It is our linear view of time that makes it appear that things are shifting from past, present, and future.

This shifting of our consciousness is happening so quickly that it appears to be a fluid motion of time. It is shifting so fast that we are not aware of it. This change in what we are tapping into in the energetic reality, that creates our physical experience, is happening billions of times per second. Because it is happening so quickly, it appears fluid. Because of the way our brains function and how we perceive time, things are not changing drastically from one moment to the next, so it appears like we are moving in linear time. In reality, we are constantly shifting from one reality to the next, over and over, very rapidly.

It is similar to when you change the channel on your television. When you see a different program on one channel, the other programs on the other channels still exist simultaneously. They are just on a different frequency. You are just not tuned into them. You can shift to different realities or timelines in this same way by shifting your energetic vibration.

Let's go back again to the example of the film at the movie theater, with the light passing through each image. They are individual frames that all exist at the same time, but as we watch the movie, they appear to be moving fluidly through time from the beginning of the movie to the end. It is the same way that our consciousness moves through each energetic potential in the field. Our vibration determines which frame on the film or which reality we are tapping into. We are tuned into what is a match to our vibration, and that creates what we experience in life.

Again, there is no time within the field. If you change what you experience as your reality of the present, then you are changing your past and future as well. There is only one moment of creation, and that is "now". This is a difficult concept for most people to grasp. However, an understanding of this will help you to know that you can shift to the realities that you prefer.

There is no reason to allow trauma from the past to affect your experience in the present and future. Shift your vibration, change your way of thinking, and shift to a reality where the past was not something that created who you are "now". The past cannot affect you, unless you create that experience of it doing so. It is only your thoughts of the memory and your imagination that are creating your current and future experience. Your memory of what happened in the past is a thought, and when you think about a past memory that caused trauma, you feel that emotion, and you bring yourself back to that vibration that matches that experience. That can lead to continuing to experience the results of the trauma and even potentially attract similar unwanted experiences.

You are in control. The Universe is all mental, so you can shift what you are creating energetically with the mind through your consciousness and change your physical experience.

If you are currently on a path leading you to being alone, in a bad relationship, struggling financially, or stuck in a career that you hate, shift to a different reality. With the knowledge that you can do this, comes the ability to do so.

Create the reality you want to experience in your mind and feel the emotion of the experience that you are creating as if it was real, because energetically it is. That will create a vibration that is a match to the experience you prefer, and then you can attract it into your life since it will be a match to your vibration.

Take your attention from what you see in your past or current experience of reality, which was created from past thoughts and emotions, and create a new reality. It is already there energetically, and as long as you have removed the resistance of the lower vibrational thoughts and emotions of what you are not happy with, the new reality will come into your physical experience. That is how the Universe works.

Who you are and what you are experiencing is constantly changing. Because most people don't focus on anything other than what they are experiencing, their experience and reality does not change drastically. If you are focused on fear and worry of what could go wrong, you may see drastic changes toward what you fear, but because you were expecting that with the worry about what you see in your "reality", it doesn't seem like a different reality. You can change to a completely different and more preferred reality if you choose to do so.

Again, because of the lower energetic rate of vibration in this physical reality, things don't happen immediately. They do energetically, but it can take time to change in our physical experience. Be patient and allow synchronicity and your intuition to guide you into a different experience of reality.

There are also multiple different dimensional realities of the Earth, as well as other planets. We are currently moving toward a shift in consciousness and a collective dimensional shift for the planet. It is up to us to choose which version of Earth we are going to exist on.

This dimensional shift of Earth is a result of the cycles that we move through. The longest cycle of the planet is the wobble of the Earth, which takes 25,920 years to complete. This is considered to be one great year in the

Mayan calendar. It is known as the Precession of the Equinoxes. This was a marker for humanity to pass in order to move human consciousness to the next level. We are obviously not through this transition, but it has started.

The starting point to measure the wobble of the Earth is when the sun is aligned with the center of our galaxy and moves through the Milky Way. It takes 36 years to move through that galactic ring, and at the time that I am writing this, we are in this 36 year cycle. The half way point in the middle was December 21st, 2012, which coincided with the end of the Mayan calendar.

If you raise your energetic vibration and tap into a world of more love and integrity, that will be available. If you are focused on the fear and all of the greed in the world, then you will stay within the current version of Earth. We are doing this collectively, but there is a great shift that is happening, and a dimensional jump will be available for those that are ready and tap into that new reality.

The multidimensional realities of Earth exist simultaneously, although with a higher vibrational rate, things will move a bit quicker. As we slowly move through this dimensional split, there will be some recognition of the others between the different vibrational realities, but as the dimensional shift moves forward and fully crystalizes, at some point you won't see those that are at a different dimension, because there will be too much of a difference in the rates of vibration. You will be living in different overlapping collective realities on the same planet.

We may complete this dimensional shift by the end of the cycle in 2030, although the time frame is fluid, as it depends on where we are at collectively, and that is always changing. It may not happen at all, if there are not enough of us to shift the consciousness into a higher dimensional reality. However, it is currently a very strong potential in the field, based on the current energies.

You may have noticed that there is more of a sense of division in the world. This is in preparation for this shift. Also, a lot of darkness is coming to the light. There is a lot of greed and corruption and bad things are showing themselves in all areas, including politics, religion, medical, pharmaceutical, big business, and more. There is a reason for this. When you see and experience what you don't want, it allows you to know what you do prefer, and then that potential is highlighted energetically in the field. Then it is there available energetically for you to tap into, once the collective consciousness and your individual vibration are high enough to allow it to come into the experience of your reality.

We are making these determinations of what we would prefer individually as well as collectively. There are many in the world that are not happy with the current state of the planet, and because of that, they are focusing on wanting to live in a more compassionate world.

There are also those that fear change and are very focused on who they think that they are, based only on their experience in this physical reality. If they continue on a path of wanting things to go back to the way they were or not change at all, then they will continue to remain in the current dimension of the planet.

Those that are collectively shifting to the higher dimension version of Earth, will be able to access more of the higher dimensional energies due to their higher energetic vibration. There will be more of a connection to the true self, more intuition, better abilities for healing, less aging, more communication with higher dimensional beings, the ability to manifest much quicker, telepathic communication, access to information learned from past lives, as well as access to all of the knowledge in the Universe.

Many people are already experiencing a strengthening in these areas as their energetic vibration is shifting higher. We are already in the process of this dimensional shift. It will be magnified much more as the collective dimensional shift of the planet is completed.

Your energetic vibration, state of wellbeing, actions, thoughts, and beliefs you have now will influence which dimensional reality that you are going to experience. Now is the time to decide who you want to be, and which collective reality that you want to experience.

UNDERSTANDING ATTRACTION

Most people are familiar with the Universal Law of Attraction, but not all people truly understand it.

Our thoughts, feelings, words, and intentions are energies, which will attract like energies. Your energy is like a magnet. What you send out in the form of energy is what you will attract back to yourself. What you experience can be perceived as good or bad, depending on what you are putting out to the Universe through your thoughts and emotions.

If you have the intent of bringing more love into your life, you can't have the belief that there isn't anyone available who is compatible for you. If you want to bring in more abundance, you can't be focused on the lack of it. If you want a new career, you can't be thinking about what you are not happy with in your current job. In difficult times, it is easy to focus on the problem, but in order to bring a positive change, it is necessary to focus on the solution or the desired outcome.

Many people will be focused on something that they want, but the wanting of it brings an awareness that they do not have it, and that creates resistance and holds them in the place of not having what they desire.

It is important to not focus on wanting something because you believe it is lacking. If you are regularly thinking about what you are not happy with or what is lacking in your current situation, you hold yourself in that vibration of what you do not want, and you are keeping yourself in that situation and also attracting additional unwanted situations of a similar vibration.

What you attract is based on your energetic vibration. If you are not happy and are thinking about what you are not happy about, then you will attract more of those lower vibrational experiences. If you are in a state of well-being, acceptance of what is, and feeling positive about the wonderful things that you can bring into your experience, then you will attract higher vibrational things that are a match to that higher vibration.

Your emotion is an indicator of your vibration. If something doesn't feel good, then it is important to look at what thought or belief is causing this resistance or energetic blockage. It may mean looking at things in a different way. In the case of having the thought or belief that what you have is not enough, you can try to look at the situation from a place of appreciation for all that you do have. If you are healthy, have a place to live, food to eat, then you are already more fortunate than many. Instead of focusing on not being happy with what is, start from that place of appreciation of the current situation. That will reduce the resistance in your energetic vibration and make it easier to create what you want to bring into your life.

If you can't come from a place of gratitude in your current situation, then remove your attention from it all together. Focus on only what you want, as if it has already happened. If you want an improved financial situation, see yourself living a life of prosperity in your mind, feel what you feel like when it happens, think of what you would do after this shift. Then with those thoughts that feel good, you are removing the energetic resistance that blocks the flow of abundance or whatever else it is that you are trying to manifest in your life.

You first need to be aware of your thoughts and feelings. This may sound obvious, but so many people are just going through their daily activities without having an awareness.

Once you have the awareness, then you need to shift your lower vibrational thoughts immediately to focus on the higher vibrational side of what you are desiring to achieve. As an example, if you want a new job, you can't focus on what you are not happy with in your current one. You need to focus on what you want to bring in. The moment you start to think about what you are not happy about, shift your thoughts to what you want to experience.

What you want to have in your life is already in the field of potentials, but it is important to remove the resistance of lower vibrational thoughts and emotions, in order to allow it to manifest into your physical reality.

You don't necessarily attract what you want, although those potentials are in the field. The vibration of "wanting" is very different than that of "having", and you attract what is a vibrational match. You can create the vibration of "having" or "experiencing" through your thoughts about what you desire, in placing yourself in that experience as if it is already happening through your imagination. Then that creates emotions that will be a vibrational match to that experience.

Remember, you only tap into what is a vibrational match to yourself. Your vibration is your point of attraction. As you change your thoughts, ideas, and beliefs, then your vibration changes, and therefore the potentials in the field that you tap into change, and then what you see and experience changes.

You have a particular way of thinking that has been with you for your entire life, and it may take time to train yourself to have that awareness, and then to shift the focus of your thoughts. Mastering the mind is the key to consciously creating everything that you want in life.

MENTAL ALCHEMY

We live in a world of polarities. Both sides of polar opposites are really the same thing, but in different degrees. There is also a balance point, although it isn't a set point on the scale, because it is all a matter of perspective. As an example, on one side of the scale is cold and the other is hot. They are both just varying degrees of the one thing, which is temperature. There is not a set line of where cold stops and hot begins. It is all a matter of perspective. It is the same with all things, low to high, or dark to light, etc. Whatever the subject is, one side of the scale is lower vibration and there is a higher vibration side of the same subject.

If you focus your attention to the more positive and higher vibration side of the spectrum, you will be able to let go of the negative thoughts and focus on what you would like to achieve, then you will attract more of what you want.

For example, if you want to let go of anxiety, focus your energy on bringing in more peace. If you want to let go of a past relationship, focus your energy on bringing in a new loving relationship that fulfills your desires. If you want to let go of financial problems, focus your attention on gaining prosperity.

If you are driving, and another driver is very rude and cuts you off, and is yelling at you, it would be very easy to have thoughts of anger about the situation. But what if you shifted your thoughts away from anger to accept that this person is either having a very bad day or just not a happy person at all, and instead react with compassion. Instead of focusing on and sending back anger to them, send positive energy and love to this person. It's not always easy to do, but it can be life changing. Remember, what you send out in the form of energy is what you receive back.

People mostly think of alchemy as turning lead into gold, but energetically it's about transforming lower vibration to higher. It is always possible to master the mind and shift thoughts to the higher vibration side of anything and transform all energies into higher frequencies.

CAUSE AND EFFECT

Every effect has a cause, and every cause has an effect. Even what may seem as random, really is not. There is a reason for everything. This is the case in the physical realm, as well as the higher dimensional realities.

On the physical realm, think about the tossing of dice, which you think brings about a random result. It really doesn't. There are specific factors that bring about the end result. There is the weight of the dice, the placement of them in your hand before you throw them, the height of where they are released from, the amount of force used in the toss, the angle and material of what they are being thrown on, etc. It is unlikely to be able to duplicate those exact circumstances, but if you could, you would get the same result.

This works with higher dimensional energy as well. Every thought and intention sets energy in motion. The "field" is constantly changing based on your shifting vibration, thoughts, emotions, intentions, and actions.

41

What you send out energetically through your thoughts, emotions, and intentions are what you attract back to yourself. If you are sending intentions of love, compassion, kindness, respect, integrity, etc., you will receive more of those in your life as well as a result. If you are sending thoughts of worry and thinking about what could go wrong, then you may not be as happy with the result of that way of thinking.

There is a cause for every effect, and an effect for every cause. Think about a past situation that you wanted to achieve something, and you accomplished it. You can go back to your thoughts, intentions, emotions, and actions to see why you were successful. The same would go for a difficult time in your life. You can go back to review your thoughts, emotions, beliefs, and actions during that time, and you will see how that created or prolonged some the unwanted events that you were going though.

There is power in knowing that you create your reality, both the good and the bad. You will know that you are the one in control.

With an understanding of this universal law, you can work to create causes that will bring about the effects that you want to see in your reality.

EVERYTHING IS IN MOTION

The Universe has a unique way of bringing balance. Everything flows in cycles. Think about day and night, the cycles of the calendar, and of the tides. If a pendulum swings one direction, it will swing back equally in the other direction.

Everything is vibration, so everything is constantly in motion. That motion creates force, and that force creates expansion and change.

We talked about the duality that we experience in this physical reality. There is a reason for this. Without sadness, you can't have an appreciation for happiness. This is the same for all things. You can't have one without the other within the physical realm because they are part of the same thing. You have an awareness of one because of the contrast of the other.

You create your physical experience through your thoughts. You create the thoughts of what you do want by experiencing what you do not want. You create by knowing what you desire, but most of that comes from knowing what you don't want to experience or don't want to continue to experience. So things can continue to shift, moving from one experience to the next.

If you experience loneliness, you create the desire for love. If you experience poverty, you create the desire for prosperity. If you have an illness, you create the desire of good health.

When you have the desire or thought of what you want to experience, then those potentials are energetically highlighted in the field. Then you just have to release the resistance though the shifting of your thoughts and emotions to allow the energetic potentials of what you desire to become a part of your reality. Then you continue to grow and create better and better situations for yourself. That is how it is meant to work.

However, many people experience what they don't want, and then continue to focus their attention and thoughts on the reality of what they are experiencing. When that happens, they are leaving themselves to continue to experience what they do not want, and they are also probably attracting other things that they don't want that are of a similar vibration.

It is important to understand, especially if you are experiencing something that you are not happy about, that everything can change, and it will, if you shift your way of thinking about it.

An example would be of a relationship that has some problems. Your partner has cheated on you, and you can't trust them. From this experience, you may determine that for a future relationship, you want someone who is loyal and who you can trust. So that is now in the field as a potential for your life, where it must be crystalized energetically first, before you can bring this into your physical experience. If you look at this bad relationship as an opportunity to bring in something much more desirable and focus on the qualities you want in a partner, then you can bring in that more positive relationship into your experience.

However, if you didn't leave the relationship because you are afraid of being alone, or don't think you can do any better, or you are focusing on what went wrong, or blaming the other person, or holding resentments about it, then you are leaving yourself in that same energetic vibration of exactly what you don't want.

There is always an opportunity for positive change. Nothing is ever static. The field is constantly changing based on your thoughts, intentions, emotions, and actions. It is up to you whether you continue with the same way of thinking and recycling old patterns that created an unwanted situation, or if you change your way of thinking to create positive changes that you can learn and grow from.

You came here to create and experience, and then create again from what you learned from those experiences, and on, and on, and on. You did not come here to get a job you don't like, a relationship you are not happy in, a life of poverty, or emotional pain, or whatever else it is, just to be stuck in that place. You are meant to, and you have the opportunity to continually experience, learn, and grow.

There should be no end to the creation of better and better things as you fine tune your desires and ability to allow these things into your experience.

HARMONY IN ALL

Nothing in the Universe is random or done in chaos. There is a harmony to nature. There are rhythms and patterns that hold everything together through a divine symmetry. The true universal language consists of mathematics, geometry, energy patterns, and frequency.

The Golden Ratio shows the geometric perfection throughout nature. It is also known as The Golden Mean or Phi. There are only two places on any line that will display this ratio. It is a powerful number present and woven into our world. Research suggests that images in this pattern impact the brain of the one looking at it in a positive way.

$$a/b = (a+b)/a = 1.6180339887488948420...$$

A Golden Rectangle is a rectangle whose side lengths are in the golden ratio. A Golden Spiral is shown when a Golden Rectangle is progressively subdivided into smaller and smaller Golden Rectangles. From this, a spiral can be drawn which grows logarithmically, where the radius of the spiral at any given point is the length of the corresponding square to a Golden Rectangle.

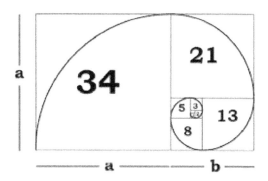

There are so many places in nature that you will find examples of this ratio. Many shells, spiral galaxies, and hurricanes are displays of the Golden Spiral. The length of our fingers, each section from the tip of the base to the wrist is larger than the preceding one by roughly the ratio of Phi. Many measurements in human bodies as well as animal bodies exhibit this proportion.

You will also find this ratio in many forms of artwork and buildings of sacred sites. It gives a visual harmony due to the perfect symmetry.

The Golden Ratio is a number that has no beginning or end. Nature is not always able to work with a number without a beginning, so it closely tries to replicate it with the Fibonacci sequence. This is another naturally occurring pattern that shows itself repeatedly.

The Fibonacci sequence is a series of numbers, where a number is found by adding up the two numbers before it. Starting with 0 and 1, the sequence goes: 0, 1, 1, 2, 3, 5, 8, 13, 21, 34 and so forth.

The Fibonacci sequence is found all over in nature. In the number of petals on some flowers, an example would be the Sunflower. It can be found in pinecones, seed heads, tree branches, and even DNA molecules.

If a Fibonacci number is divided by its immediate predecessor in the sequence, the ratios are converging upon one number, Phi. This occurs from both sides of the number. As the ratios of the numbers in the sequence get larger and larger, the ratio will eventually become extremely close to the Golden Ratio.

$2/1 = 2$ (bigger)
$3/2 = 1.5$ (smaller)
$5/3 = 1.67$ (bigger)
$8/5 = 1.6$ (smaller)
$13/8 = 1.625$ (bigger)
$21/13 = 1.615$ (smaller)
$34/21 = 1.619$ (larger)
$55/34 = 1.618$ (smaller)
$89/55 = 1.61818182$ (bigger)

Not only are there patterns that repeat throughout nature and the Universe, but there is geometry that everything is based from. Every element in the in the periodic table of elements is connected to one of the five platonic solids, as is every cell in our body, so our very nature is geometrical in origin. These five geometric shapes are the keys to all physical creation.

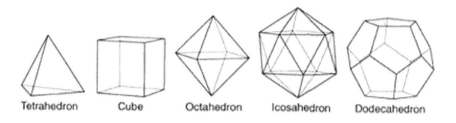

Tetrahedron   Cube   Octahedron   Icosahedron   Dodecahedron

Each of the platonic solids have the same face shape on each side and the same angle per edge. If you spin any of these five shapes around its center point, its corners will create a perfect sphere.

The platonic solids, which are the geometric structures that create all matter in the physical Universe, are found in sacred geometry in Metatron's cube. Metatron's Cube has a relationship to the Flower of Life, which is a representation of the energetic vibration of All That Is.

The Tree of Life of the Kabbalah is also a part of the Flower of Life, and it is said to be a map of All That Is. It represents a map for consciousness from a vibrational level, but also represents the path used in the creation and direction for all worlds in all dimensions.

The Flower of Life symbol is a representation of All That Is, and it has been found all over the world, with some images possibly being over 10,000 years old. Within it are the symbols of the Seed of Life, which represents the central starting point and creation of All That Is. The Egg of Life is also a part and represents the start of all physical life, and it is also seen in the first cells of the body of every living being. The Fruit of Life is said to be the blueprint of the Universe, containing the design of every atom in existence.

Sacred geometry symbolizes the architecture of the Universe, the collective consciousness, and All That Is. It is said to be the fingerprint of God.

There is a connection with geometry and pattern within the harmony of music as well. The ancient Greek philosopher and mathematician, Pythagoras, combined music and geometry into a tuning system. This tuning system, with A = 432 Hz, contains the sum of the angles of each of the platonic solids as well as the sum of the angles of the 2D geometric shapes as well.

Historically, music appears to have always been tuned to 2nd A note 432 Hz. It was changed to be standardized to 440 Hz in 1938, and there are some conspiracy theories that this was done intentionally to cause discord.

432 Hz is said to have healing properties due to the fact that it resonates in harmony with nature. The difference in the effect of the two different frequencies upon water crystals is visible. Your body is approximately 70% water, so you can imagine what a difference it can make in the body as well.

If you add the degrees of each of the corners of each of the platonic solids, you will see that they are all multiples of

3,6, and 9, and if they are reduced to a single digit they add up to 9. This is the same for the 2D basic geometric shapes, and 432 as well. All of the 60 individual notes in the Pythagorean A = 432 Hz scale are divisible by 9, and if reduced to a single digit (example: 4+3+2=9), they will also add up to 9.

Music tuned any other way loses the mathematical and geometrical synchronicity. The entire tuning chart is in synchronicity with the Universe as defined by 2D geometry, 3D geometry, sacred geometry, and a surprising number of terrestrial and extra-terrestrial measurements. 432 Hz is said to be the natural frequency of the Universe.

If you play a note based on the sums of the angles of the circle, triangle, square, pentagon, hexagon, and septagon, together you will get a F# major cord. If you do the same thing with the 3D versions of these geometric shapes, you will get the same naturally perfect major cord.

Keep in mind, that each of the notes corresponds with one of the chakras, the energetic centers of the body. The F is the heart chakra, and there for the half step of the F# would be the high heart chakra, which is between the heart and throat chakras, and is the first connection of the higher self to the physical body.

If you take the sums of the basic geometric shapes and apply the Fibonacci sequence, you will also get a numerically perfect major chord. If you apply the Fibonacci sequence to vibration cycles, the first six numbers will always present a numerically perfect major chord. This shows that that harmony is what anchors every Fibonacci series.

- Tetrahedron (4 interlocking triangles) - 180° sum of the internal angles x 4 sides = 720 / 3rd octave F#

- Cube or Hexahedron (6 interlocking squares) - 360° sum of the internal angles x 6 sides = 2,160 / 5th C#

- Octahedron (8 interlocking triangles) - 180° sum of the internal angles x 8 sides = 1,440 / 4th F#

- Dodecahedron (12 interlocking pentagons) - 540° sum of the internal angles x 12 sides = 6,480

- Icosahedron (20 interlocking triangles) - 180° sum of the internal angles x 20 sides = 3,600 / 5th A#

Here are the total degrees of the angles of the basic two dimensional geometric shapes, which are also included in this A = 432 Hz. tuning system.

- Circle- 360°
- Triangle- 180°
- Square- 360°
- Pentagon- 540°
- Hexagon- 720°
- Septagon- 900°
- Octagon- 1,080°

The number 432, within this tuning system, is considered a sacred number as well. The author and teacher, Joseph

Campbell claimed it to be the most important mythological number in history.

It is a number connected to Precession of the Equinoxes, which is the largest cycle of our planet. There is a connection to this cycle and the potentials for higher consciousness. This shift in consciousness is what is going to take humanity to the next dimensional level where we will have the opportunity to create a more compassionate world and expand our abilities to much greater levels.

The Precession of the Equinoxes, which was previously mentioned, is the wobble of the Earth that is caused by the rotation of the Earth's axis. It is responsible for the slow movement of the earth through the 12 zodiac constellations. It takes 25,920 years to complete this cycle. The starting point to measure the wobble is when the Sun is aligned with the center of our galaxy and moves through the Milky Way. It takes 36 years to move through that galactic ring, and at the time of writing this, we are currently within this 36 year cycle. The halfway point was December 21st, 2012, which coincided with the end of the Mayan calendar.

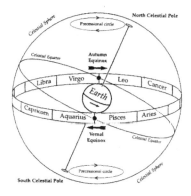

Here are some other places where the sacred number of 432 comes up:

- 2,160 years (25,920 being one great year) would be one great month (25,920/12), which is also the time to move through each sign of the zodiac- 216 x 2 = 432

- 2,160 miles is the diameter of the moon- 216 x 2 = 432

- 21,600 breaths per day- 216 x 2 = 432

- 86,400 heart beats per day- 864/2 = 432

- 864,000 miles is the diameter of the sun- 864/2 = 432

- 86,400 seconds in a day- 864/2 = 432

- 360 degrees in a circle x 12 = 4,320

- 432 squared = 186,624 (which is in within .01 percent of measuring the speed of light)

All of these numbers, including the sum of the angles of the platonic solids and the basic two dimensional geometric shapes, the time of the wobble of the Earth, the cycle to move through the Milky Way, and the speed of light are all divisible by 3, 6, and 9, and will add up to 9 if reduced to a single digit. Remember the quote from Tesla "If you only knew the magnificence of 3,6, and 9, then you would have a key to the Universe".

If you have a circle with the numbers 1-9 equally spaced around the circle. If you join the lines of 3, 6, and 9, you will see a triangle, and that again shows the connection of geometry within the Universe.

The number 9 is also a very sacred number. In Hinduism it is the number of the creator. For Hebrews, it is a symbol of truth. It is said to be the number of completion and fulfillment. If you add up the numbers 1 – 8, you get 36, which is again divisible by 3, 6, and 9, and reduced to a single digit is 9. The number 9 contains the energy of all other numbers within it, so it also represents a connection to all.

It is not necessary to focus on the numbers, symbols, and mathematics, but the point is that absolutely everything is connected through a divine symmetry and that there is harmony to everything. What appears to be random, is by design, a divine system of benevolence and love.

The ancients were very aware of this connection of All That Is to geometry, numbers, vibration, and sound. Somewhere along the line, this information was lost, and it is now the time to be re-discovered. All That Is, is a divine system of love, and we are all a part of it.

SUMMARY OF KEY #1: UNDERSTANDING HOW THE UNIVERSE WORKS

- Everything is energy. This energy is created of subatomic particles that are affected by consciousness and are not limited by space or time.

- There is an energetic field that everything that exists is a part of. Everything and everyone are connected by this field. This is All That Is, and it is a combination of consciousness and vibration. We are part of the divine oneness of All That Is.

- We are much more than who we experience ourselves to be within our temporary "vehicles" in our physical experience. We are eternal beings of light, created from and a part of All That Is.

- Time and space are not as fixed as they appear in our experience. Our "reality" is an illusion. It is the experience that is real, and we are creating our experience through our consciousness, which is guided by the higher dimensional part of ourselves.

- The larger part of who we truly are remains in non-physical form and helps to guide our experience though our intuition and emotion. We also have the assistance of other higher dimensional beings.

- Everything exists as potentials in the energetic field. Our consciousness determines which of these potentials are tapped into through our thoughts, and therefore our thoughts create the reality that we are experiencing.

- Our reality is a mirror of our consciousness. What we experience is a reflection of our vibration, which is a result of our thoughts and emotions.

- Everything is crystalized energetically before we can experience it in our physical reality.

- There is only one moment in creation. Everything exists "now". If you change what you experience as your reality of the present, then you are changing your past and future as well. As we tap into each moment in the field, we are shifting into new realities and new versions of ourselves.

- We are in the process of a collective dimensional shift of the planet. As our collective consciousness continues to rise, we are creating a higher dimensional version of the Earth. The current version of our planet will simultaneously exist along with higher vibrational version. Our energetic vibration will determine which version will experience.

- Our thoughts, feelings, words, intentions, and actions are energies, which will attract like energies into our life experience.

- You don't necessarily attract what you want, you attract what is a vibrational match. Your energetic vibration is your point of attraction.

- We live in a world of duality. There are higher and lower vibrational sides of everything. Both sides, even though they may be opposites, are the same thing, just in varying degrees of vibration.

- When we experience or have an awareness of what we do not want, it creates the opportunity to have an awareness of what we do want, and that is then a potential for us to experience in our physical reality.

- Every effect has a cause, and every cause has an effect. Even what may seem random, really is not. There is a reason for everything.

- You came here to this physical realm to create and experience, and then create again from what you learned from those experiences, and on, and on, and on.

- Nothing in the Universe is random, it is all by design. It is all vibration, and can be expressed through geometry and mathematics.

- There is a harmony to everything within a divine system of love.

Key #2:
Raising Your Energetic Vibration

WHY IS OUR FLOW OF ENERGY IMPORTANT?

When we talk about the energetic vibration, it is all about the flow of energy. The higher your vibration is, the less energetic resistance you have. Your natural state is of the highest vibration and is in alignment with your higher self. It is the blockages from lower vibrational thoughts and emotions that cause the energetic vibration to drop. All you have to do is let go of what is not in alignment.

With less energetic resistance, created by lower vibrational thoughts and emotions, you can easily connect to higher dimensional energies. That would include your higher self, so you would have a better guidance system to lead you to the highest potentials for yourself. Your intuition would much stronger and you can manifest everything you desire much quicker. Your higher vibration would be a match to attract higher vibrational opportunities and situations from what is in the field of all potentials.

Your energetic vibration also affects your overall

wellbeing in all areas mentally, emotionally, spiritually, and physically. When you are not holding onto negative beliefs, thoughts, and emotions, you remove all resistance, so energy can flow freely.

With a higher energetic vibration, you are at peace, feel balanced, happy, healthy, and are in alignment with the higher dimensional part of yourself. With such a state of wellbeing, you are thinking more positively, focused on everything you have to be grateful for, and what you want to improve your life even more. With those positive thoughts, you are drawing more positive experiences from the field into your reality.

Your energetic vibration is the most important factor in creating the life you desire! You attract what you are a vibrational match to. When energy is flowing, you are in a state of allowance, and are open to receiving all of the wonderful things you want to manifest into your experience of life.

HOW DO WE RAISE OUR VIBRATION?

We each have a standard rate of vibration, and we shift up and down from that point. If we are having a good day, we are a little higher than our average vibration, and if we are having a bad day, we will drop a bit.

While your vibration is always shifting, it takes time to shift from your normal rate of energetic flow. You usually will not go from an exceptionally low vibration to a very high vibration immediately, or visa versa. It is just too much of a jump. You just raise and fall around your average vibration.

The goal is to raise your standard vibration, so that your average vibration is very high. Then when something you perceive as bad happens, if you allow it to affect you, your vibration drops just a little bit. If you are just dropping a little bit from a higher point, then you are still in a good place.

If you are at a place where your average vibration isn't

where you want it to be, be patient. This probably isn't going to change overnight. Big vibrational changes, in either direction, usually take some time. The more awareness that you have and the more of these techniques that you implement, the quicker you will reach the higher vibration that you want for yourself.

There are many tips and tools to raise the energetic vibration. There is not only one path, but the more of these practices that you incorporate, the better.

MEDITATION

The first way to raise the vibration, that many are familiar with, is meditation. This is a very powerful tool, and not only does it help to improve the flow of energy, but it helps to reduce stress, anxiety, provides emotional balance, and allows for the receiving of spiritual guidance.

There a many different ways to meditate, so if one doesn't work for you, try something different. It is a way to clear the mind, which sounds very simple, but it may take some practice. If you can't simply just quiet the mind, and many people can't, there are different meditation techniques to try.

You can try different breathing techniques or just focus on the breath. There are guided meditations that take you on a journey thought the mind. You can chant or repeat a mantra or sound. There are walking meditations, where you are just being mindful and aware of your breath and every step you take, bringing you into the present moment.

Anything that allows you to clear your mind can be a meditation. Some people are in a meditative state as they run or workout, some people clear their mind while gardening, or creating art or music. It doesn't matter how you clear your mind of thought, only that you do.

This helps raise your vibration because you are not having the random thoughts that are constantly going through your mind which are creating energetic resistance.

In order to provide an ongoing and lasting effect from meditation, it is important to be consistent. Try to meditate for 20 minutes every day. In the morning is usually best, because it's a nice way to begin the day. Although, it can be helpful to do it in the evening as well, so you can let go of all of the stressful thoughts from your day.

Many people feel that they are too busy to make time for meditation, but that is when they need it the most.

FEEL JOY

It was previously mentioned that the feeling of joy is one of the ways that your soul speaks to you. Do the things that bring you that feeling of joy and happiness. When you are in that state, your energy is flowing, and you are in a state of allowing for more of what makes you feel happy.

People can get so caught up in what they have to do in

their daily lives, that they don't prioritize what brings them joy. I know there is work, cleaning, bills, laundry, and all of the other things that have to be done, but it is very important to make time for what makes you happy.

When you are happy in life, it is contagious. You can have a positive effect on those you care about. You are also going to have a better flow of energy that will allow you to have more vitality and motivation, so you will be more efficient. If you are just doing what you need to do, and not feeling any enjoyment, then you will become fatigued and drained.

You should never feel guilty about taking the time to enjoy life. You didn't come into this physical realm just to work and do chores. You came here to create and experience all you desire!

The feeling of joy is also a way that the higher self is guiding you to your highest potentials. It is an indication that you are in alignment. If you follow that feeling, you will be headed in the right direction.

CONNECTING WITH NATURE

The Earth has a way of soothing the soul. It is very healing to take the time to connect with nature. Especially, if you are in a place of mindfulness, being present in the moment, to really feel the healing energy from our beautiful blue planet.

There is so much beauty in nature! You can watch the sunset, or take a walk along the beach, hike to a waterfall, or whatever else you may feel drawn to. Maybe even just sit in your backyard, feeling the sunshine and gentle breeze, with your feet in the grass, and breathe in the fresh air.

It can be very grounding and peaceful, and it allows you to disconnect from the stress of daily life. If you quiet the mind, you can feel the connection to The Earth and all of the living beings that we share the planet with.

GRATITUDE AND APPRECIATION

Take time to feel the appreciation for the things that can be easy to take for granted, like your health, family and friends, that you have a place to live and food to eat. Feel gratitude for even the little things, like a beautiful sunset, a song you enjoy, or a delicious meal. The more feelings of gratitude you have, the easier it is to attract more things that will give you that same feeling of appreciation, because what you are sending out to the Universe in the form of energy is what you will attract back to yourself.

Every time you feel appreciation for something, you are reminding yourself of the things that you feel good about, which brings you to a higher state of wellbeing and higher vibration.

With every thought of appreciation, you are telling the Universe "more of this, please".

SPENDING LESS TIME WITH ELECTRONICS

It is also beneficial to take time to disconnect from the electronics, as they are distractions, and they can keep the mind occupied with things that are not positive. This would be the television, cell phones, computers, video games, etc.

Disconnect from the news occasionally, as it is usually promoting fear and separation. That doesn't mean that you have to live in a bubble and be unaware of what is happening in the world. It just means that it is good for you not to have your focus there constantly.

The reality of "what is", if it is not desirable, is not where you want to focus too much of your attention. Think about the reality that you would like to see, perhaps a world with more integrity and compassion.

Also, there is much sadness in the world that you may be aware of as you are watching the news. You can send energy of compassion, and you can do what you can to help, if you are in a position to do so. You do not have to, and you should not take on the sadness of the world. That does not help anyone. It is a choice. You are able to be in a better place to help by maintaining a higher energy vibration.

It's easy to get caught up into. I know that I sometimes feel it and have to be aware and shift my way of thinking, especially when I come across those commercials with children and animals who are suffering. Feeling sad does not help anyone.

The solution to any situation is not found by focusing on the problems. It is found by focusing on the potential solutions and the desired outcome. I donate money to organizations that are making a positive impact. We have a rescue dog who we give as much love as possible to. I would help them all if I could, but I know that I am doing what I can. I also work energetically with the planet and those in need by working with my intention and energy to send more love and light to all, and I always do my best to be an example of the love and compassion that we all are at the soul level.

Working on ourselves to raise our vibration and consciousness is the best way that each of us can help others as well. Your higher vibration can be an example for other people, and it can also allow them to utilize that higher vibrational energy to potentially match closer to. The elevation of our vibration affects the elevation of human consciousness as a whole. If you allow yourself to feel sadness or anger at what is happening in the world, that is affecting your energy, which affects what you experience in life, and it is not helping anyone.

MINDFULNESS

It can also be beneficial to be in the present moment as much as possible. Much of people's time is spent focusing on either the past or the future, and they are missing out on the only moment that really exists, which is now.

So many people live in the past. They go over things that

have happened in their mind, over and over. They try to analyze what happened, try to figure it out, think of what could have been different, hold onto emotions caused from a past situation, or use the past to place blame on others for their current situation or feelings.

The past no longer exists in your life, because there is only "now". Only memories of the past exist, and those are thoughts that you are bringing up in the present. Those thoughts of the past memory are creating the same vibration of the past experience, and that vibration is creating what you experience in life.

Remember, as you are moving through each moment, you are shifting into new realities. Your future is not created from a past experience. It is created from the thoughts in the present that you are focusing on from that past experience. If that is not the reality you prefer, then shift your thoughts to a reality that is what you would like to experience, and then the past experience shifts along with it.

The present is where you create from, and that includes the creation of your past and future, as well as your beliefs about who you are as a person now. You can create from your current thoughts of memories from the past, but you do not have to, it is a choice.

The future does not exist yet in your experience either. There is only your thoughts or worries about what may happen in the future. If you worry about what horrible thing may happen, you may experience what you don't want, and then you justify those thoughts, because the reality you created showed you that you had reason to worry. Then you continue down that same way of thinking.

That doesn't mean that you shouldn't think about the future, because you can create it as you would like. The key is to know that you are always creating your future from the thoughts you are having in the present. So, be mindful of what those thoughts are, so you can create the future you want to experience instead of the future you are worried about.

Don't be so caught up in the past or future that you are missing the only moment that is real. Be present in your thoughts, right now. Don't allow random thoughts to distract you from what is happening. Pay attention to what you are doing, how you are feeling, and what you are thinking.

If you are eating dinner, really taste and enjoy every bite of delicious food. If you are taking a walk, notice the beautiful scenery with each step. If you are having a conversation with a loved one, really pay attention to what is being said. If you are hugging someone, feel the warmness and the connection.

If you find yourself being distracted by a busy mind, just have the intention to clear your mind and come back into the present moment. It can help to focus on your breath and feel your consciousness at your heart center. Just breathe and be aware of what you are experiencing, thinking, feeling, and doing right now.

MOVING THE BODY

You can also raise your energetic vibration with movement of the body. It doesn't need to be a strenuous workout. It can be as simple as getting outdoors and walking around the neighborhood.

Gentle movements that also combine mindfulness and focused breathing, such as practices in yoga, Qigong, or tai chi are especially beneficial because they are combining several different techniques that raise the energetic vibration.

Dancing is another form of movement that helps lift the energy in some, or it may be running for others. It doesn't matter how you do it, but you just want to make sure that it feels good to you, and that it doesn't feel like a chore.

EATING HEALTHY

What you eat can also make a difference, not only for your physical heath, but for your energetic vibration. Meat, along with foods that are processed, fried, sugary, or heavy have a lower vibration. Fresh fruits and vegetables have a higher vibration.

You can feel the difference. When you are eating those heavy foods, you probably won't feel your best. When you are eating more fruits and vegetables, you feel energetically lighter.

OPENING YOUR HEART

When you are living with an open heart, that lifts your energy higher as well. It's easy to get caught up with feeling your consciousness as your brain, but that isn't the part of you that is connected to your higher self. The brain is only a receiver and transmitter. It is meant to allow you to experience physical reality, but it isn't meant to guide you or connect you to your higher self.

Your heart center is a connection to the higher vibrational part of yourself. With a stronger awareness of that part of yourself, you are more aligned with who you really are. When you understand that you are so much more than this physical body, you become aware of your true power. This brings a sense of peace with that knowing.

When you are more aligned with your higher self, there is less energetic resistance to block the flow of energy. You allow yourself to be guided in the right direction, and you develop a sense of trust. You connect with feelings of joy, love, and compassion. These are all emotions that are of a high vibration.

It is easy to bring your consciousness to your heart, just by having the intention to do so. Take a moment to think of something that brings that feeling of love to your heart center. If you are a parent, this may be a memory of your child when they were young and happy. It may be an image of a fur baby that is so happy to see you when you get home. It may even be as simple as a beautiful image of nature. Just take a moment to really feel that love at your heart center.

Slowly breathe in and out as if you were breathing from the heart. Feel that warmth at your heart center expand.

WORKING WITH CRYSTALS

Everything is energy, and our energy is affected by the energy of everything and everyone around us. Because of that, the stable and high vibration of crystals can have a positive effect on our energy as well.

A crystal is defined as a solid, that the atoms or ions that compose it are arranged with a "highly ordered" repeating pattern due to the periodic arrangement of the atoms in three dimensions. Because of this highly ordered geometrically perfect structure, the energetic vibration of the crystal is very stable and will usually be of a high energetic vibration.

The stable vibration will help to balance our own energetic vibration. Also, our energetic vibration will be increased if we are near the higher vibration that is coming from the crystal. Just like a tuning fork will start to match to another that is close to it, our energy vibration can become a closer match to a higher vibration that is close by.

My husband and I own a metaphysical store, which is basically a crystal shop with some other wonderful items that are available as well. I personally use crystals in multiple different ways to help keep my energy flowing.

Selenite is wonderful for cleansing lower vibrational

energy that causes energetic blockages. I have a big piece that I sit on when I do readings for people. I have a big piece at home in front of the couch to rest my feet on. I have a piece on the headboard of my bed. I use crushed Selenite in a bath along with salts to help keep me energetically cleansed.

We also have a crystal bed that I utilize, and our customers love it as well. It is using Quartz crystal Vogel points that are aligned above each energy center of the body as you are laying on a massage table. Clear Quartz is known as a master healer. Pulsing color light moves through the crystals that are aligned with the chakras. This is another tool that I use to keep my energy flowing and my vibration as high as possible.

If I am feeling off, or just not quite myself, I will often feel drawn to hold onto a crystal or throw one in my pocket. I can usually feel the shift in my energy in a short time.

We will talk a bit more about crystals and how to select, cleanse, program, and use them in other sections in this book. Not only can they help to raise your energetic vibration, but there are crystals that can help in working with the chakras which are main energy centers in the body, and they can also assist in the manifestation process.

SOUND VIBRATION

The vibration of sound is very effective in moving through the body and helping to move through lower vibrational energy that is blocking the flow.

In our store, which is also a healing studio, we use all kinds of different sound healing tools. We have gongs, crystal singing bowls, Tibetan singing bowls, tuning forks, crystal pyramids, and drums. Some of our bowls are so big, that you can stand within them, and feel the vibration moving all though the body. We host sound baths and also offer private sound healing sessions. They have been extremely popular, with our sound baths selling out months in advance, because those attending can really feel the difference.

I also work with sound vibration within the Reiki energy healing sessions, and I work with Reiki energy within the sound healing sessions and baths. They work very well together.

The lower frequencies of depression, disease, stress, anger, or whatever else it may be, can be raised by matching to a higher vibration. Sound vibration is one of the ways to accomplish this. However, if the person goes right back to the same way of thinking about things, it will only be a very temporary fix.

Each chakra has a corresponding musical note as well, so you can use the sound vibrations from either tuning forks or singing bowls to help clear and balance each chakra. The notes for each chakra are listed on the upcoming pages with information for each energy center. Again, because our energy is affected by energy, a vibration near will give the body the opportunity to match closer to it, bringing the chakra back into balance.

The vibrations coming from a singing bowl are very uniform and symmetric, so when you fill the bowl with water, you can see the order that is produced from the vibrations. Now, once again, realizing that your body is approximately 70% water, imagine what it can do to bring your energy back in balance, which will raise the energetic vibration.

Everything is vibration. Nothing in the Universe is random or done in chaos. There is a harmony to nature. There are rhythms and patterns that hold everything together. When you can utilize some of those harmonic frequencies that are found in nature, that will also help to bring harmony to the energetic body. We have already previously discussed the healing power of the frequency of 432 Hz due to the resonance with the natural patterns of the Universe.

The Solfeggio frequencies also correspond to the harmonics of the Universe. They have been utilized since ancient times for the purpose of healing, bringing the body into balance, and raising the energetic vibration. The Solfeggio frequencies make up the ancient 6-tone scale that was used in sacred music, including the Gregorian Chants and ancient Indian Sanskrit Chants.

These are the Solfeggio frequencies and what they have been claimed to do:

- 396 Hz- Eliminates guilt and fear

- 417 Hz- Facilitates change

- 528 Hz- Transformation and miracles (DNA repair)

- 639 Hz- Brings love and compassion

- 741 Hz- Awakens intuition

- 852 Hz- Connects to the higher self

Each of these frequencies if added and reduced to a single digit will be a 3, 6, or 9. Remember what Tesla said about those numbers being the key to understanding the Universe.

ENERGY HEALING

I mentioned the Reiki energy healing sessions that I offer, but there are many types of energy healing. It is all utilizing the same energy that surrounds and connects us all, along with the intention of wellbeing. Everyone can tap into this energy and utilize it for the healing of self, for others, and for the planet.

The first thing that I let people know in the healing class that I teach is that the most important part of becoming a successful healer is to make sure that they have done the work to raise their own vibration first. Not all healers are equal, and anyone can take a class that lasts a day or two and receive a certification. That does not mean that they have done the introspective work to make sure that their energetic vibration is as high as possible. The higher your vibration, the better of a healer you will be, because the energy will flow through you better and you will be aligned with higher dimensional energy. If you are having a healing session done yourself, make sure that the healer that you selected is not dealing with their own energetic problems. They should be an example of peace, balance, joy, and compassion. With an awareness, you can usually tell who has a high energetic vibration and who still has work to do.

The word Reiki is made of two Japanese words "Rei" which means "God's Wisdom or the Higher Power" and "Ki" which is "life force energy", so Reiki is actually "spiritually guided life force energy". It is the intention of the healer to work with the energy to help move through blockages, and provide a higher vibration for the person being healed to match to if they choose, and to allow higher dimensional energy to flow through.

A healer is not the one doing the healing, but they are providing a higher vibration of wellbeing for the individual to match to, so that they can heal themselves. If they have a belief that it is not going to work and are not open to the experience, they most likely will not receive the benefit. If they are open to receiving the benefit of a higher vibrational energy, that will help to provide the desired outcome.

Usually in a healing session there are many different techniques that I will utilize. I work with higher dimensional beings of light that help assist in the healing sessions. I can feel the higher dimensional energy flow through my body, and it is then directed to where the person needs it. I will usually feel my hands move to exactly where a person is having a problem, even if they did not let me know about that specific problem beforehand. I also visualize each of the main energy centers or chakras, and see the color getting brighter and expanding. With my intention I will move bright white light through the body, that helps to release energetic blockages. I will also usually receive telepathic messages about what the person that is in the healing session needs to be aware of and what they can do to help themselves. Towards the end of the session, I will also incorporate sound healing, and I will play the singing bowls and other instruments. I will set the bowls directly on the body to help move through energy even more, improving the flow and vibration.

While there is a lot that you can do on your own to raise your energetic vibration, it can definitely be helpful to see an energetic healer as well. Just know that any energetic blockages, which are the cause of all problems, were caused by your own thoughts and emotions. If you go right back to the same way of thinking, then your energy flow and vibration will go back to the way it was before the healing session. It is important to take responsibility for your energy and know that ultimately you are the one in control of all aspects of your physical experience.

AWARENESS OF RESISTANCE

The most important thing that you can do to increase your energetic vibration is to be aware of the beliefs, thoughts, emotions, and behaviors that are creating energetic resistance, and shift them. In the next sections of this book, we will go into information on how to do the introspective work to become aware of those areas of resistance, and how to let go of those thoughts and beliefs that are holding you back from your highest potential.

ENERGY FLOW THROUGH THE CHAKRAS

We have already talked a little bit about the chakras, which are the energy centers that connect higher dimensional energies with the physical body. While it isn't necessary to know which energy center has a blockage that is caused by a lower vibrational thought or emotion, it can help some people to work through the energies with this awareness, so we will provide some information on these energy centers.

The Sanskrit word "chakra" literally translates to "wheel" or "disk", and the chakras are clockwise spinning energy centers in your body. These energy centers are connected by lines of energy, and they are the receiving points of energy within your body.

There are many energetic points in the body, but there are seven main chakras that have a major effect on you in your physical reality. The flow of energy through the chakras greatly affect your mental, emotional, and physical health.

Our chakras are affected by energy. This energy can be caused from within, through your own thoughts and emotions, or they can be affected by receiving energy from the universal energy field that connects us all.

If someone near you is angry, that can influence your personal energy, if you allow it to. You are the one in control of your energetic vibration, and outside sources can not have a negative effect unless you allow it to through your own thoughts and feelings.

In our store, we have many people coming in looking for crystals, candles, or sage to protect themselves from other people's energy or bad intentions for them. If people believe that there is negative energy being sent to them or that is surrounding them, and it is going to have a negative impact on them, then that is the experience they are creating for themselves. I always let them know that they are creating the problems that they have been experiencing themselves, so that they know that they are in control and can change the way that they are thinking.

You attract that which you are a vibrational match to. If you are feeling a lot of negative energy around you, work on raising your own energetic vibration, so that anything lower isn't a match, and therefore cannot have an effect. If you feel negative energy in your space, think of something that brings that feeling of love at your heart center, and with your intention imagine sending that feeling of love through the space. You can also envision filling the space with white light to raise the vibration.

If you are having thoughts and feelings of lower vibrational energies, such as fear, worry, stress, anger, guilt, sadness, etc., then this can cause blockages in your energy centers, which affects the flow of energy through your body, and therefore affects your energetic vibration.

Lower vibrational energy needs to be cleared in order to raise your energetic vibration. With lower vibrational energy, you will feel unbalanced, emotional, and if you hold onto these lower vibrational energies too long, it will affect your physical health. The higher your vibration, the better your mental, emotional, and physical health will be.

The chakras at the lower part of your body, spin slower than the chakras at the upper part of the body. Also, the lower chakras correspond more with the physical world, and the upper chakras affect spiritual issues.

I will provide some information on each of the main chakras, but please keep in mind that the most important thing is to shift your thoughts and beliefs to allow energy to flow freely. It is not necessary to know which chakra is blocked, although it can be helpful for some.

THE CHAKRAS

ROOT CHAKRA (Muladhara)

Symbol:

Color:
Red

Location:
Base of the spine

Relates to:
Physical security, safety, and survival

Element:
Earth

Musical Vibration:
Key of C

Crystals:
Garnet, Obsidian, Black Tourmaline, Hematite, Onyx, and Red Jasper

Essential Oils:
Rosemary, Ylang-Ylang, Myrrh, Frankincense, Benzoin, Patchouli, and Sandalwood

Foods:
Cherries, pomegranate, beets, watermelon, red apples, and strawberries

Unbalanced Root Chakra:
It can lead to feelings of being a victim, depression, fear, insecurity, stress, a lack of self-confidence, and anxiety.

Health issues related to Root Chakra:
Physical imbalances may manifest as problems in the colon, with the bladder, kidneys, with elimination, or with lower back, leg, or feet issues. In men, prostate problems may occur. Eating disorders may also be a sign of a root chakra imbalance.

Recommendations:
Connecting with nature, walking barefoot in the grass, or swimming in a natural body of water

Affirmations:
I am grounded, balanced, and centered with a sense of well-being.

My spirit is grounded in the material world.

I feel the stability that the Earth provides.

I have all that I need.

I am in control of my life, trusting that all my needs are met.

SACRAL CHAKRA (Svadisthana)

Symbol:

Color:
Orange

Location:
Just below the navel

Relates to:
Physical desire, emotions, passion, and creativity

Element:
Water

Musical Vibration:
Key of D

Crystals:
Carnelian, Amber, Orange Calcite, Peach Selenite, and Sunstone

Essential oils:
Orange, Bergamot, Neroli, Clary Sage, Rosewood, and Patchouli

Foods:
Oranges, mangos, carrots, pumpkin, nectarines, and apricots

Unbalanced Sacral Chakra:
It can lead to feelings of self-pity, feeling guilty or shameful, feeling deprived of enjoyment, and emotional unbalance.

Health issues related to Sacral Chakra:
Physical imbalances may manifest as problems in the bladder, kidneys, reproductive system, menstrual problems, sexual disorders, addictions, weight gain, and sexually transmitted diseases.

Recommendations:
Maintaining a gratitude journal, doing something that brings you joy, or buying something special for yourself

Affirmations:
I am celebrating an enjoyable life of abundant pleasures and gratifying experiences.

I feel blessed, and I feel gratitude for all the joy in my life.

I value and respect my body.

I am open to feeling passion in my life.

SOLAR PLEXUS CHAKRA (Manipura)

Symbol:

Color:
Yellow

Location:
Just above the navel

Relates to:
Self-confidence, self-worth, inner strength, will power, and empowerment

Element:
Fire

Musical Vibration:
Key of E

Crystals:
Citrine, Tigers Eye, Pyrite, Yellow Jasper, Goldstone, Topaz, and Agate

Essential oils:
Lavender, Rosemary, Clary Sage, Roman Chamomile, Spikenard, and Patchouli

Foods:
Bananas, squash, lemons, pineapple, corn, yellow peppers

Unbalanced Solar Plexus Chakra:
It can lead to feelings of insecurity and fear, feelings of not being worthy, being controlled or manipulated by others, fear of rejection, or a lack of self-respect.

Health issues related to Solar Plexus Chakra:
Physical Imbalances may manifest as problems in the liver, digestive issues, and problems with the immune system.

Recommendations:
Physical exercise, completing goal or project, or teaching others about empowerment

Affirmations:
I am empowered with respect and honor for myself.

I love and accept myself.

I stand up for myself.

I am strong and courageous.

I am worthy of love, kindness, and respect.

HEART CHAKRA (Anahata)

Symbol:

Color:
Green

Location:
Center of the chest

Relates to:
Love, compassion, relationships, and healing

Element:
Air

Musical Vibration:
Key of F

Crystals:
Rose Quartz, Aventurine, Emerald, Bloodstone, Rhodonite, and Pink Calcite

Essential oils:
Rose, Neroli, Melissa, Eucalyptus, Ylang Ylang, and Jasmine

Foods:
Salad, avocado, kiwi, green apples, broccoli, spinach, and celery

Unbalanced Heart Chakra:
It can lead to difficulty in giving or receiving love, feelings of vulnerability, not being capable to have intimate relationships, not being able to forgive.

Health issues related to Heart Chakra:
Physical Imbalances may manifest as problems in the heart, circulatory, immune, or respiratory systems.

Recommendations:
Sharing love with someone in need, provide an act of kindness, and social activities with friends or likeminded people

Affirmations:
I am open to receive love in all forms.

I forgive the past and open my heart to love.

I am connected with other human beings.

I feel a sense of unity with nature and animals.

I feel compassion for all of humanity.

THROAT CHAKRA (Vishuddha)

Symbol:

Color:
Blue

Location:
Throat

Relates to:
Communication, expression, and speaking your truth

Element:
Sound

Musical Vibration:
Key of G

Crystals:
Blue Lace Agate, Sodalite, Lapis Lazuli, Angelite, Aquamarine, Turquoise, and Blue Calcite

Essential oils:
Lavender, Geranium, Eucalyptus, Sage, Jasmine, and Peppermint

Foods:
Blueberries

Unbalanced Throat Chakra:
It can lead to difficulty in expressing thoughts and feelings, fears of rejection, not being able to communicate honestly, or a repression of creative expression.

Health issues related to Throat Chakra:
Physical imbalances may manifest as problems in the upper respiratory and digestive systems.

Recommendations:
Communicating your true thoughts, ideas, or beliefs, or any type of artistic expression, such as painting, writing, drawing, music, or photography

Affirmations:
I am open, clear, and honest in my communication.

I communicate my feelings with ease.

I express myself creatively through speech, writing, or art.

I am speaking, living, and expressing my truth.

THIRD EYE CHAKRA (Ajna)

Symbol:

Color:
Indigo

Location:
Center of the forehead

Relates to:
Intuition, imagination, and psychic abilities

Element:
Light

Musical Vibration:
Key of A

Crystals:
Sodalite, Labradorite, Moldavite, Iolite, Azurite, Lapis Lazuli, Amethyst, and Sugilite

Essential oils:
Bay Laurel, Palo Santo, Myrrh, Sandalwood, Nutmeg, German Chamomile

Foods:
Blueberries, eggplant, plums, blackberries, and black grapes

Unbalanced Third Eye Chakra:
It can lead to difficulty in listening to your inner truth, and overanalyzing and over thinking everything within your reality, and an inability to trust your intuition and therefore having a feeling of uncertainty or confusion.

Health issues related to Third Eye Chakra:
Physical Imbalances may manifest as problems in the nervous system, memory issues, lack of concentration, and headaches.

Recommendations:
Meditation, attending spiritual workshops or lectures, yoga, spiritual art, automatic writing, or listening to inspirational music

Affirmations:
I am in touch with my inner guidance.

I listen to my deepest wisdom.

My intuition allows me to make the best choices for my highest good.

I am connected to the wisdom of the Universe.

CROWN CHAKRA (Sahasrara)

Symbol:

Color:
Purple

Location:
Top of the head

Relates to:
Spirituality, consciousness, connection to the Universe and all living beings, your soul purpose

Element:
Consciousness

Musical Vibration:
Key of B

Crystals:
Amethyst, Clear Quartz, Selenite, Moonstone, Ametrine, and Sugilite

Essential oils:
Frankincense, Sandalwood, Rose, Lavender, and Spikenard

Foods:
Eggplant, plums, blackberries, purple grapes, and cabbage

Unbalanced Crown Chakra:
It can lead to confusion, greed, a feeling of isolation, and a lack of awareness of everything greater than oneself.

Health issues related to Crown Chakra:
Physical Imbalances may manifest as problems in the nervous system, mental disorders, psychosis, and learning disorders.

Recommendations:
Meditation, prayer, connecting with nature, visualizing sending healing energy to the planet and all living beings, yoga, and visiting sacred places

Affirmations:
I am one with the Universe.

I am connected to all living beings.

I channel universal wisdom to bring peace, love, and harmony to the world.

I am much more than my physical body.

I am the Divine, I am Source, and I am an eternal being of light.

Now that there is an understanding of each chakra, we can go into specifics on how to release blocked energy from these energy centers. This would be anything that holds back the flow of energy and therefore our energetic vibration, which affects everything. When I say everything, I am referring to your wellbeing in all areas (mental, emotional, spiritual, and physical), your ability to manifest what you want in your life, and your ability to receive information from your higher self.

Here are some tips on how to raise your vibration through working with the chakras.

MEDITATION

During meditation is an excellent time to work on the chakras. In our store, I lead weekly guided meditations, and in most of them, I include a chakra clearing exercise.

Here is a chakra balancing meditation that you can use if you would like. You can record yourself as you read it out loud, and then you can play it back for a meditation when you feel like you need some chakra clearing and alignment.

At the end of the meditation, you may want to use an automatic writing technique of just seeing what comes to you without any thought, just putting the pen to paper and seeing what comes though. It may surprise you. If you don't receive anything the first time, don't give up on the technique. You can always try again another time. Make sure that you have a pen and paper ready, so you don't have to go searching for one after the meditation. There is also space to write in this book after the meditation, so you can review this information that came through for you at a later time as well.

Close your eyes and relax your body. Take a deep breath in, filling your lungs to the top with air, and slowly release. Slowly, deeply, and rhythmically breathing in and out. If you are breathing in for 5 seconds, then breath out for 5 seconds. Continue at your own pace that feels comfortable for you. Slowly breathing in, and slowly breathing out.

Imagine roots coming from the bottom of your feet, slowly moving into the Earth. They are moving through different layers of soil all the way down into the core of the Earth. You can feel the magma at the center of the Earth, but it doesn't hurt or feel uncomfortable. You are deeply connected with the Earth. Just feel the connection. Feel the stability that this connection provides.

Feel your consciousness at your root chakra, at the base of your spine. Visualize a ball of spinning energy, as a beautiful vibrant red color light. This beautiful ball of energy is spinning clockwise, and just feel it moving at your root chakra. Watch it expanding bigger and bigger. See the color get brighter and clearer, and see the movement spinning faster. Just focus on this beautiful color at your root chakra. Know that this is helping you to feel grounded. Know that you have everything that you need. Release all stress, fear, and worry that you are holding onto within this chakra, down through your body, down through the branches, and down into the center of the Earth to be transformed. Now see the movement of this beautiful red ball of energy moving even faster, getting bigger, and brighter.

Now, feel your consciousness at your sacral chakra, just below your navel. Visualize and feel the ball of spinning energy as a beautiful bright orange color light. See and feel it spinning at your sacral chakra. Watch it expanding bigger and bigger. See the color get brighter and clearer, and see the movement go faster. Just focus on this beautiful vibrant orange color at your sacral chakra. Know that this is helping you to feel joy, passion, and excitement. It is also helping you with creativity and allowing you to manifest the life you desire. Release any feelings of guilt, shame, or anger that you are holding onto within this chakra, down your body, down through the branches, and down into the center of the Earth to be transformed. Now see the movement of this beautiful orange ball of energy moving even faster, getting bigger, and brighter.

Feel your consciousness at your solar plexus chakra, just above your navel. Visualize and feel the ball of spinning energy as a beautiful bright yellow color light, like the color of the sun. See and feel it spinning at your solar plexus chakra. Watch it expanding bigger and bigger. See the color get brighter and clearer and see the movement going faster. Just focus on this beautiful bright yellow color at your solar plexus chakra. Know that this is helping you with self-confidence, inner strength, and willpower. It is allowing you to know your own inner power. Release any feelings of insecurity or of not being completely happy with who you are down through your body, down through the branches, and down all the way into the center of the Earth to be transformed. Now see the movement of this beautiful yellow ball of energy moving even faster, getting bigger, and brighter.

Feel your consciousness at your heart chakra, right in the center of your chest. Visualize and feel the ball of spinning energy, as a beautiful emerald green color light. See and feel it spinning at your heart center. Watch it expanding bigger and bigger. See the color get brighter and clearer, and see the movement go faster. Just focus on this beautiful bright green color at your heart chakra. Know that this is helping to open yourself up to giving and receiving more love in all forms, including self-love. It is allowing you to feel more compassion for every living being. Release any emotional pain from past experiences that you are holding onto within this chakra, down through your body, into the branches coming through your feet, and down into the center of the Earth to be transformed. Now see the movement of this bright green ball of energy moving even faster, getting bigger, and brighter.

Feel your consciousness at your throat chakra. Visualize and feel the ball of spinning energy as a beautiful blue color light. See and feel it spinning at your throat chakra. Watch it expanding bigger and bigger. See the color get brighter and clearer, and see the movement go faster. Just focus on this beautiful bright sky blue color at your throat chakra. Know that this is helping you in all areas of communication. It is allowing you to freely express yourself and communicate your truth. Release any fears of rejection or of not being accepted due to your thoughts, beliefs, or for just being yourself, down through your body, though the branches, and down into the center of the Earth to be transformed. Now see the movement of this beautiful blue ball of energy moving even faster, getting bigger, and brighter.

Feel your consciousness at your third eye chakra, right in the center of your forehead. Visualize and feel the ball of spinning energy as a beautiful indigo, blue violet color light. See and feel it spinning at your third eye chakra. Watch it expanding bigger and bigger. See the color get brighter and clearer, and see the movement go faster. Just focus on this beautiful indigo color at your third eye chakra. Know that this is helping you to enhance your intuition. It is also helping you to be able to trust your inner guidance. Release any fears about not making the right decisions for your future that you are holding within this chakra, down through your body, down through the branches coming from the bottom of your feet, and down into the center of the Earth to be transformed. Now see the movement of this beautiful blue violet ball of energy moving even faster, getting bigger, and brighter.

Feel your consciousness at your crown chakra, at the top of your head. Visualize and feel the ball of spinning energy as a vibrant royal purple color light. See and feel it spinning at your crown chakra. Watch it expanding bigger and bigger. See the color get brighter and clearer, and see the movement go faster. Just focus on this beautiful purple color at your crown chakra. Know that this is helping you with your spiritual connection. It is also helping you to feel the connection to all living beings and to realize that you are part of something much bigger than yourself. Release any feelings of isolation or separation that you may be holding onto within this chakra, down through your body, down through the branches, and down into the center of the Earth to be transformed. Now see the movement of this beautiful royal purple ball of energy moving even faster, getting bigger, and brighter.

Now see a cord of bright white sparkling light reaching from the top of your head all the way up to the highest point in the universe that you can imagine. There is a part of you energetically connected from high up in the universe all the way down to the center of the Earth. Visualize a beautiful ball of energy, the same energy as the cord connecting you to the higher realms. Visualize this bright white sparkling ball of light coming down through that energetic cord, down through your crown chakra at the top of your head, down through your third eye chakra, through your throat chakra, to your heart chakra, to your solar plexus, down through your sacral chakra, to your root chakra, and down through your legs, down the bottom of your feet, and down into the center of the Earth.

This beautiful source energy has helped to clear your chakras even more and allow for a better flow of energy through your body, to allow for a higher energetic vibration, that will allow for a happy, healthy, and balanced life.

106

Whenever you are not feeling balanced and centered, you may work with your chakras with your intention to help bring yourself back to a state of well-being.

Align with your higher self. You may see this as a ball of iridescent bright white light, with a brighter light at the center. Allow this energy to merge with your physical body. The bright light in the center of this beautiful energy will align with the light at your heart center. You may feel like it clicks in place. Just breathe and feel this connection.

Ask for guidance regarding anything you need to know about what you need to let go of, or how to release what may be holding you back from your highest potential and your highest energetic vibration.

When you are ready, slowly open your eyes. Without any thought, put your pen to the paper, and allow information to flow through you from your higher self. You may be surprised at the insights that you receive.

AUTOMATIC WRITING / CHAKRA BALANCING

.

INTENTION AND VISUALIZATION

The chakras can be cleared and balanced through intention. We did this in the meditation, but you can also do it as a short exercise in the morning when you first wake up, or any time that you are feeling off balance.

You can visualize the chakras, focusing on the movement, size, and color of each energy center. See the matching color of spinning light at the location of each chakra, and see the movement getting faster, the color getting brighter, and the energy expanding.

Then visualize energy being able to freely move through each chakra. You can do this by visualizing a bright white light coming down from the highest point you can imagine, and pouring over and through your body, moving all the way from the top of your head and down through the bottom of your feet and into the center of the Earth. This is a high vibration energy. The white light is very bright, you can think of the color of lightning.

WORKING WITH CRYSTALS AND OTHER TOOLS

You can also use crystals help in working with your chakras. Because of their geometric perfection, they hold a higher vibration that will affect your personal energy when they are close to your physical body.

There are listings of crystals to use for each chakra in the previous pages with the details for each chakra. Many of the crystals recommended to use to clear and balance a particular chakra have colors that correspond to that chakra. This is because color is an energy and holds its own vibration. This isn't always the case though, because sometimes it is the energy for the crystal and not the color. An example would be that Rose Quartz is an excellent heart chakra crystal, and the color relating to the heart chakra is green, but Rose Quartz is a light pink color.

You can lay the crystals for each chakra right on each chakra point, or you can hold them in your hand with your intention to clear and balance each chakra or a particular chakra.

Selenite is very good for clearing lower vibrational energies, so you can use this crystal to help clear blockages. There are bath salts, soaps, and body scrubs with Selenite that can help clear your energy and raise your vibration.

It works not only with the energy of the crystal, but also your intention to work on opening the chakras as well. If you are working on opening your heart chakra, and you have a small Rose Quartz crystal that you are working with to assist with that, every time you pick up that crystal or even put your attention on it, you are also sending your intention out to the energetic field of all potentials to heal this energy center.

A crystal is a wonderful tool to help you move through energetic blockages and open the flow of energy, but it isn't going to do all of the work for you. Many people come into our store and think that a crystal is going to magically fix all of their problems. They may have been told by a healer or a psychic that they have a blocked chakra, and they want a crystal that will fix it, without having a real understanding of what the problem is or what is causing it. It can help along with other techniques, but if you continue to hold onto the same beliefs and thoughts that caused the problem in the first place, it is not going to change anything.

You can also work with your intention through the use of other tools, such as candles, oils, or incense to help keep the chakras open and balanced. There are particular colors and fragrances that are specific for each chakra, and these are noted in the pages with the information listed for each chakra.

SOUND VIBRATION

The vibration of sound is very powerful in helping to move through energy blockages of the chakras. We have already discussed how it can be utilized to help improve the flow of energy and raise the energetic vibration.

In working specifically with a particular chakra, you can utilize the resonating note for that chakra to help to bring it into balance, the power of sound vibration to move through energy, or you can utilize the other frequencies that are in harmony with nature to help bring the energy and body back into balance.

AFFIRMATIONS

Stating affirmations is an immensely powerful way to create change as well. Your intention is the most positive creative life force there is, and it is so much more powerful than most people realize.

In order to be able to express your intention, that means that you are very clear in what you want to achieve. You are focused on what you want, rather than focusing on what you do not. You are coming from a place of power.

There are affirmations listed under the pages with information for each chakra. You can create your own as well. You want the words and the energy behind those words to resonate with you and your intention.

WORKING WITH COLOR

Color has its own energy that corresponds with each of the chakras. You can tap into the energy of that color to help bring a chakra back into balance.

You can do this with the color of the foods you are eating, the clothes you are wearing, or the color of a crystal you are working with. The crystal bed at our store utilizes colored light that moves through Quartz crystals for amplification.

Not only are you tapping into the energy of the color, but as you are noticing the color that you have chosen to work with, you are also utilizing the power of your intention and thoughts to create a specific outcome.

ENERGY HEALING

We previously spoke about energy healing, but this is also an effective way to help clear energetic blockages within the chakras. If you are being treated by a healer who is in touch with the Universe, they will be able to sense where energy is not flowing or is building up and causing problems.

An energy healer can open the door for you to be able to heal yourself, but it is very important to do your part as well. It is up to you to match to a higher vibration, no one can do that for you, so you need to open yourself to it and have the intention for healing.

Also, once you are aware of a problem, it is up to you to determine what belief or thought is causing it, and then shift your way of thinking to be more in alignment with your true self.

INTROSPECTION

The most important part is to do the introspective work to realize what lower vibrational energies that you are holding onto, and then release these energies by no longer allowing them to have an effect on you. Let them go.

116

WHAT DO YOU NEED TO LET GO OF?

It isn't as important to know exactly which chakra that you need to balance, as it is to know what beliefs and thoughts that you need to shift. You can choose to connect the chakra with the lower vibrational energy if you would like, but it is not necessary.

The first step to letting go, is to be aware of what you need to let go of. So many people are so focused on the day to day things that they have to deal with, that they are not even aware of what they are holding onto that is holding them back.

Lower vibrational emotions and feelings are the indicators of areas that thoughts or beliefs need to be looked at and shifted. If something doesn't feel right, then don't just ignore it. Pay attention and look at what beliefs and thoughts are causing those feelings. Everything you experience in life is neutral, and only has the meaning that you give to it. We are the ones that assign meaning to any situation.

There can be a positive to come from any experience if you look at the situation in a positive way, and maintain a state of wellbeing, no matter what happens. Sometimes an experience you don't prefer happens to help guide you to something that you do prefer to experience. It can be an opportunity to open you to something better or to learn something that will help you as you move forward. You can't always control a situation, but you can control your response to a situation, and that is where your power is. A positive outcome can only come from a matching state of wellbeing.

Here are some of the possibilities of what may need to be released, but self-introspection is the key.

Root Chakra-
Fear, stress, financial concerns, worry, anxiety, insecurity, concerns about the future.

Sacral Chakra-
Guilt, anger, resentments, jealousy, issues regarding sexuality, shame, depression, lack of gratitude, self-pity, lack of joy or passion.

Solar Plexus Chakra-
Lack of self-confidence, lack of inner strength, fear of rejection, feelings of not being worthy, lack of self-respect, not having will power.

Heart Chakra-
Grief, sadness, emotional pain, anything that needs forgiving, inability to give or receive love either for others or yourself.

Throat Chakra-
Not being able to communicate clearly, not being able express yourself without holding back, or speak your truth, not living your truth or hiding parts of yourself because you care about other people's thought or opinions, or not living the truth of who you are as a soul being.

Third Eye Chakra-
Lack of trust of the intuition and higher self, overthinking, feelings of uncertainty.

Crown Chakra-
Greed, selfishness, limiting beliefs, lack of connection, feelings of isolation or loneliness, or the lack of understanding that you are more than a physical being.

It will be important for you to look at your life and determine what you are holding onto that is holding you back by lowering your energetic vibration. It is very important not to focus too much on these lower vibrational thoughts, but if they are already there, it is necessary to have an awareness in order to shift them.

Do not get to caught up into them. If you could only focus on the higher vibration side of what you want to create for your reality without putting any attention on what is lower vibrational, that would be ideal. Unfortunately, many people are already being affected by their thoughts in a negative way and need to have the awareness of how to shift those energies.

Before you start working on your own introspective work, I want to provide some examples from my own life. This may be able to help some people understand a little better. I also want everyone to know that if I can shift my vibration from where I started at my lowest point to where I am now, anyone can do it. This was life changing for me, and I hope that sharing my experience will help provide hope to those who may need it.

When I was much younger, about 30 years ago, I was struggling financially. I was a single parent of a very young child. My mother had passed away when I was 19, and I had a baby at 20. This was by far the most difficult period in my life.

I felt completely alone, and I felt abandoned by friends and family. Because it is difficult to be around anyone who is struggling and not be willing to help, I had many people exit my life. I was asked to leave my father's house, and I was having the most difficult time in every way possible. Not only was I responsible for my own survival, but I was responsible for my young child's wellbeing as well.

This was a time of all kinds of energetic blockages. I was in a complete state of fear. I was working very hard and long hours in retail, but not making very much money. Because I was working irregular hours and weekends, my childcare expenses were very high. I was nearly homeless.

After paying for a place to stay and childcare, there was not much money for anything else. There were times that I only had $20.00 a week to feed myself and my son.

Because I couldn't afford the deposit for an apartment, and didn't have great credit, I was living in a hotel for quite some time. At one point, because of unexpected costs to keep my car running, I didn't have the money to pay for the hotel, and I wasn't going to get my paycheck for another three days. I called my brother and explained my situation to him and asked if my son and I could stay with him and his family for three nights, and I was told that it wasn't a good time, while I was crying on the phone.

I had to call my dad and ask him if my son and I could stay there for three nights, and if he could help to loan me a few dollars until I got paid. I was told no at first, and then I was very reluctantly told that I could stay there for three nights. I was working long hours and had a long drive to my son's child care and my work, so I was going to be away from 8:00 AM – 8:00 PM, so I really only needed a place to shower and sleep, but this was apparently too much to ask.

So I drove to the house that I grew up in, with little gas in my car, just praying that I would make it there. It was pouring rain and my son and I were both sick. I didn't make it. I ran out of gas about ten minutes away from my dad's house. I just barely made it to the gas station, but I didn't have any money to buy the gas. So, again I had to call my father. I sat in the covered front entrance of an El Torito restaurant to keep cover from the pouring rain. We waited there for hours. There was a nice couple who came out of the restaurant, and they noticed that I was waiting there as they were going in, and they asked if there was anywhere they could take us. I had to tell them that I had nowhere to go.

Eventually my father showed up, and in front of my son, who was about 3 years old at the time, was telling me how stupid I was and how I just waste money. He did give me money for some gas, and we went to his house to sleep. His new wife did not like me at all, and I felt the same about her. I have never felt so unwelcome anywhere in my life, and this was the home I grew up in. I had a fairly normal childhood with a mother who I was very close to, in an upper middle-class family. Money was never an issue when I was growing up, so this was a completely new experience for me.

I gave my son a half a glass of orange juice from the refrigerator, making sure not to use the last of it. That became a huge issue. This was so strange to me, because it really hadn't been that long since I left home at that point. I was in my early 20's at that time. My parents were very generous. They donated time and money to different charities and were very generous with friends and family. My friends were always welcome to make themselves at home at our house and were welcome to eat or drink anything we had available.

Once I received my paycheck, I went back to the hotel that I was staying at. I was looking at apartments, and the man who was showing them to me offered to help me to cover the money that I was short for the deposit personally.

However, that would have taken all of my money and I didn't get paid for another week. He offered to take us out to dinner a couple times during the week to help, and he said that he was sure that my family wouldn't let us starve. Unfortunately, I didn't have those same certainties. I had to turn down the offer, so that I could be absolutely certain that I could feed my son. I was very touched that a total stranger was willing to help me though. We continued to bounce from hotel to hotel for quite a while barely getting by, until another man that I didn't know very well offered to let us stay with him, which had its own set of problems, which ultimately provided some more lessons to learn from.

I look back at this period in my life, and I can see clearly all of the lower vibrational energies that I was holding onto. I knew at the time that my life was a disaster, but I didn't know that I could shift it all, and that I was in creating my own reality. I didn't come to that realization until years later, so even though things got a little better from that point, I still struggled for many years.

Here is a breakdown of what I needed to realize that I was holding onto, so I could make a conscious decision to shift those thoughts and beliefs to help me to release the lower vibrational energy and bring me into alignment with my true self.

Root Chakra-

I was always worried about money and survival. This was not anything that I ever had to worry about until my mother had passed away. Without her, I felt very vulnerable, and was full of fear of not being able to support myself or my child. Because I had these worries, I ended up creating a reality that reflected my worst fears.

In order to shift that, I had to make a conscious decision to let go of fear. I came to the realization that fear and worry don't help anything, and they only make things worse. I had to know that I could do what I could, and that was all that I could do. I came to a place of acceptance of my situation, and I made a decision to heal myself and change my life. I felt guided to learn as much as I could about energy, and I read a lot.

I saw myself in a better place financially, before it became a reality. I thought about what positive changes that I wanted to see in my life. I stopped thinking about what my reality was, and I shifted my thoughts to what I wanted my reality to be. I also meditated every evening to help bring me to a place of peace and balance.

This wasn't an overnight fix, but as I worked on myself through self-reflection and shifting my thoughts and feelings, things gradually got better and better. I was able to get better jobs, and eventually did quite well.

For quite some time, I still felt that I had to work really hard to maintain it, and I had to shift that belief as well. I spent much of my son's childhood working very long hours, instead of finding balance between my work and personal life. It wasn't until later that I was able to understand that I could do more energetically than through long hours of work, and once I accepted the new belief, I was able to bring my life back into balance and focus more on what is truly important.

Sacral Chakra-

This is the center of joy and gratitude. I was so focused on just surviving, that I really didn't even focus on anything joyful. I had just accepted it wasn't possible for me to be happy.

So, I had to decide to think differently. I worked on gratitude and shifted my thinking to not be focused on my financial issues and all of the other issues in my life that I wasn't happy about. I focused on what was good, even when I had to really search for the smallest thing to feel appreciation for. I looked for the pretty flower, a beautiful sunset, a smile on my son's face, a delicious bite of food, or a great song to feel good about.

Happiness can't be conditional. You can't think that you will be happy, once your finances improve, or you are in a good relationship, or whatever else it is that you want. Your life is a reflection. The mirror isn't going to smile at you, until you smile first. I had to decide to be happy first, or at least work on it with baby steps until I truly could be happy.

Solar Plexus Chakra-

This is your power center, and during that time of difficulty in my life, I felt completely powerless. I lost my self-confidence because I felt like I was failing at life and not being able to give my son everything that he deserved.

I had to accept myself for who I am, regardless of how anyone else felt about me. I decided that even if there wasn't anyone else in the world that cared about me, that was fine. I looked at who I was as a person, and decided that I was happy with who I was. I was kind, thoughtful, honest, intelligent, and I was doing the best that I could to be a good mom.

I came to a place of acceptance that I didn't have people who cared about me in my life. I had myself and my son, and that was all I needed. I decided to stop feeling sorry for myself. I decided to stop looking for happiness from outside sources, and to find it within myself. I decided to stop looking back at difficult things that happened, and I made a decision to be present and look forward with a knowing that I could create a better life for myself and my son.

I started to become more independent. I decided that I wasn't going to wait for someone to invite me to do things that I wanted to do. I was going to do them anyway, even if it meant doing them by myself. It took a little getting used to, but I came to enjoy myself, and even appreciated not having to worry about what anyone else wanted to do. I could eat where I wanted to eat. I could travel where I wanted to visit. I could do everything I wanted to do, and I didn't need anyone else.

Once I came to a place of happiness on my own, then I could focus on what types of relationships that I would want in my life. It's not possible to create a happy relationship while being sad about being alone. It isn't a vibrational match. In order to manifest a healthy relationship, I had to be at a state of well-being of my current situation so that I could have the energy behind my desires that were of a higher vibration.

Also, as I was going through this introspective process, I could see exactly what thoughts and feelings brought me to where I ended up in life. I was willing to take responsibility for my life, and also accept my own power to change it.

Heart Chakra-

The death of my mother had a huge effect on me. I cried every day for months when she passed away from cancer. I was filled with sadness. Because of this energetic blockage at the heart, I wasn't able to open myself emotionally to any relationships, while at the same time I felt very sad, alone, and unloved.

In order to move through this, I had to shift my belief about death. When my mom died, I did not realize that there is no such thing as death, and that there is only transition. In all the reading and learning that I was guided to through my intuition, I came to that understanding. I would attend mediumship demonstrations and see the healing that would happen for people as they received messages from their loved ones in spirit. There were always tears and laughter. Even though I never received a message myself, it was helpful in showing me that consciousness and love exist beyond death of the physical body. I had to look at death in a different way.

I decided if it was possible for people to communicate with those that had passed over, that I was going to do everything I could to be able to connect with my mom. I continued my studies about energy and mediumship and the importance of raising the vibration, and I got to the point that I could receive messages from higher dimensional energies.

I no longer felt sad about my mother's death. I was focused on our continued connection. I focused on the love and not on the loss. It was life changing, like a weight had been lifted.

Since then, I have lost other people that I was very close to, and I was able to move through it without any sadness at all. I was even able to feel happy due to their transitions.

I received the message that the more love you give, the more you will receive. I worked with my intention to send love to the world and every living being, especially for those who needed it the most on a daily basis. I still do this regularly to this day. We also do this as a group within the healing circles that I lead at the store.

Once I was able to open my heart, then I was not only able to release the sadness that I was holding onto for so long, but I was also able to open myself to have healthier relationships. Not only romantic, but friendships, and better relationships with family. I felt more of a sense of peace.

Throat Chakra-

This chakra had been a problem for me since childhood. I still have difficulty with public speaking, but as a child, I rarely spoke to anyone other than those who I was very close to. If a classmate would say hello as they ran into me in the grocery store, it was difficult for me to even say hello back. I didn't want to be rude, but I just was so uncomfortable talking, and that would drive my mom crazy. Even just reading out loud in front of the class would give me a lot of anxiety and that sick feeling in my stomach.

I have had to really work on my throat chakra. I would have never thought that I would be able to communicate through writing books, teaching classes, or leading healing circles, but I did it anyway, even when it wasn't comfortable. By expressing myself, I was able to open myself up more, and open the flow of energy.

Being someone whose beliefs are not the same as most people can be difficult. I communicate with higher dimensional energies, I work in a field that is considered ridiculous by many people, and some people even feel that the work that I do is evil, even though it is all based in love. I had to be able to live and speak my truth, and not care about what anyone else thought.

Before I opened our metaphysical store with my husband, I was working as a product manager for a very Christian sunglass company. They would gather every week as a group and take turns reading from the bible. They were all very nice people who I liked very much, even though we didn't have the same spiritual beliefs. When I made my decision to leave my job to open the store, I let them know what my plans were, and everyone there was very supportive. I was concerned that they would think what I was doing was wrong, but everything was fine, and they even asked me to stay and work from home as a contractor, which helped me very much as we were first growing our business. I also had to let my family know, and that was a side of me that they did not know about.

I never should have felt that I needed to hide that part of myself, but that was something that I had to learn. Ultimately, if they didn't accept me because of my beliefs and who I really am, it would have been alright for them to fall out of my life anyway.

I wrote my first book "Working with Energy", and I and came out of the spiritual closet so to speak. With our store, we have those unusual discussions every day, and it is wonderful. I work to provide a safe space for everyone to have to talk about those things that they may not be comfortable talking to their co-workers or family about just yet.

Third Eye Chakra-

My third eye has always been one of my most open chakras. I have always had a sense of knowing, and my mom said that she knew that I was psychic from the time that I was about two years old.

However, in that very difficult time in my life, energy wasn't flowing. I didn't have a sense of knowing. I was feeling that I was on my own to make decisions through logic rather than knowing what to do and where to go. I felt very lost and confused.

When I finally came to a place of acceptance, then I was able to be more open to that inner guidance of what to do next. It took some time to be able to trust it completely, but now I live my life and make all decisions based on my intuition without hesitation. It has worked out quite well.

Crown Chakra-

When I was younger, I didn't have a spiritual connection at all. I was open, but wasn't sure if this life was all there is. When my mom had passed away, I was looking for signs from her, but never received any, until many years later. In fact within a couple of years, I had lost my mom, all of my grandparents had passed away, as well as a close family friend. I kept looking and wishing for signs, but there was nothing.

Nearly 15 years later, that is when I started receiving signs that led me to believe that there was life beyond death and that there is more than our physical existence. There were flashing lights, knocking sounds, coldness out of nowhere, smells of perfume, and I had even sensed a tapping on my shoulder when there was no one anywhere around me. It wasn't just once in a while, it was happening many times a day. There was someone trying to get my attention.

One day my son had left the television on in the room after he finished a program, and there was a show with a medium on who was giving messages to someone from a family member that had passed away. The pure emotion that was being shown led me to believe that this may actual be a real communication. That is when I started reading, attending classes, and going to mediumship demonstrations to learn as much as I possibly could.

Once I had experiences of my own and learned through others as well that there is no such thing as death, I was able to view life with a much larger view and understanding. As my beliefs shifted, then I was more open to receiving communication from higher dimensions. First, I developed a communication system through the signs I was receiving, flashing lights were "yes" and knocking sounds were "no". Then I started using a pendulum, then oracle cards, then automatic writing, and then I realized that none of that was needed because I was receiving information telepathically.

I kept learning and growing, and my perception of life had shifted completely. My crown chakra is now my strongest.

There are so many more experiences that I could share about my own introspective work, and how I needed to shift my way of thinking to move through those lower vibrational thoughts and emotions, but I think this is a good representation to show some examples and inspiration.

Not only was I affected mentally, emotionally, and spiritually due to my state of energetic vibration that was caused by my thoughts and emotions, but it was also affecting my physical health. In those difficult times, I had bad back pain, a cough that lasted years, I was prone to pneumonia, and I was in a state of constant fatigue.

I have gone from a life of difficulty, sadness, pain, and struggle to a life that I never could have dreamed of. I am happier than I could have ever imagined was possible. I went from thinking I would be alone forever to having an amazing relationship with my wonderful husband. I went from being nearly homeless and barely being able to feed myself and my child to having all of our needs met and beyond, including being able to do incredible things like travel the world. I went from being in meaningless jobs that were very unfulfilling to loving my work as a healer, teacher, author, and everything we are doing with our business, The Sacred Journey. I went from no longer wanting to live to being in love with my life.

Anything is possible! Doing the introspective work and raising the energetic vibration is necessary in order to manifest everything you desire into your experience.

So now it is your turn to list what you need to let go of. I am leaving some pages in this book for you to write on. This is a book that you may want to review more than once, and it can be very powerful to reflect back and see where you were successful in letting go of what is holding you back from your dreams, or where you need to do a bit more. If you need more room, you can use other paper or a notebook to list these things that may need to be looked at. In writing them down, it will help you to bring clarity to yourself.

Remember, you don't want to dwell too long on these areas of problems. The goal is not to focus too long on what is problematic. However, sometimes we are holding onto things that need to be shifted in order to be released, so that they can no longer hold you back.

WHAT I NEED TO LET GO OF:

HOW TO LET GO

Now that you know what you need to let go of, we will go through some tips on how you can do that. Depending on what you are dealing with, it may not be an overnight shift. That is ok. You most likely won't jump from a low vibration to a very high one immediately. It is just too far apart, but you can get there. Just by bringing yourself to a place of awareness is a huge first step that many people don't ever think to take.

WORK WITH YOUR INTENTION

The key is to work with your intention to accept and release what you are ready to let go of. That does not mean suppress and ignore them, while still allowing them to affect you. It means consciously making a decision to let them go, and no longer allow these things to negatively affect you.

Your intention is much more powerful than most people realize. This is a way to indicate to your higher self what you really want to achieve.

LOOK FORWARD INSTEAD OF LOOKING BACK

From our perspective in physical reality, the past is behind you, and it cannot be changed. Many people dwell on it though, overthink the situation, try to understand it, or wonder what could have been done differently. It would be better to be able to accept it for whatever it is, acknowledge the lesson learned, and focus their attention on what is ahead, and what they want to bring into their life.

Remember, we only experience our life with a past, present, and future because of our physical reality. Everything exists energetically in one moment, now. Because of what we were focused on in what we experience as our past, we brought specific experiences into our reality. However, now we can tap into a different potential that has nothing to do with what we previously tapped into, to create a completely different experience for ourselves in the future.

The past cannot create what you experience in the present and future. It is only the thoughts you have about what happened in the past that are creating your experiences in the present and future. When you focus on a memory from the past, you bring back that emotion from the experience, and that same energetic vibration from that time. That will hold you in that same place of wellbeing or a lack of it, and it will also attract other experiences that are of a similar vibration.

You can decide who you want to be for the future. You don't have to allow any past circumstance to have any effect at all. Tune into who you want to be, and then shift your beliefs, thoughts, and behaviors to match that vibration. Everything exists now, so you can shift to a different potential than what led you to what you are currently experiencing in life. Use your imagination to tune in and allow your higher self to guide you to that new reality.

YOU ARE NOT A VICTIM OF CIRCUMSTANCE

It is important to know that unhappiness or any other state of being that you are experiencing was not caused by circumstances. Your state of being and what you are experiencing is a result of your own mind, based on your beliefs and thought patterns, which create your emotions and feelings and determine your behaviors. It is your beliefs, thoughts, emotions, and behaviors relating to these circumstances that created your energetic vibration, which is the cause of what is being reflected back in your physical reality. The result is your current life experience.

It doesn't matter what happened. It is your beliefs, thoughts, emotions, and behaviors about what happened that create your state of being and vibration, and therefore what you are experiencing. Nothing has meaning in itself. You determine your beliefs about any circumstance, as well as your state of being.

SHIFT YOUR THOUGHTS

It may be necessary to shift your thoughts or beliefs about something in order to let go and move forward. Going back to the example of when my mother passed away many years ago, I was devastated. When I changed my thoughts about death, and realized it was not a death, but a transition, I was able to let go of the sadness and the pain. I was able to focus on the continued connection, rather than the loss.

Here is another example that occurred later. I was working as a Senior Development Manager for an action sports apparel company. I wanted to move up in the company to a Director position that had opened up. However, I wasn't happy in my job and I did not respect my boss. So, leaving myself in this position wasn't really what was best for me, but at that time, gaining the title was important to me, even though my salary was already in the range of what Directors were making. The title was just a word, and it wouldn't have changed my job at all. Once I was able to let go of my thought that a title was important, I was able to move on to work at a different company, making the same salary, and I had more independence to do things the way that I wanted to, and I was much happier.

At the time that I started writing this book, we had to close our store due to the Covid-19 pandemic. While, I have done the work, and it usually isn't a problem for me to look at everything in a positive way, this actually took a little effort for me to shift my thoughts. My main concern was that we had thousands of dollars going out each month, and nothing coming in. I knew those thoughts would lead to an outcome that I did not want. I had to shift them, to focus on having trust that we would have enough money to hold us over, that the stimulus programs would help, and this was actually a positive situation. I had time to go outside and meditate every morning, we went on family walks around the neighborhood every evening, we ate at normal hours since we weren't working, I had time to put an online store on our website, and I had the time to finally start writing this book. There were so many positive things to come out of this, and I just had to shift my thoughts to those positive aspects and the outcome I desired. We made it through perfectly fine, without any negative financial impact, and since we have our online store now up and running, this will help us to reach even more customers out of the area for future growth.

Another example is in readings that I have done, I have come across people who were not willing to leave an abusive relationship or situation because they didn't want to lose their house and nice car. I've never had my happiness depend on those things, so it was difficult for me to understand that way of thinking. I was perfectly happy when I was living alone in my small studio apartment. If this person was willing to let go of the belief that it is important to have a big house, they could have let go of a toxic relationship, and moved forward being much happier in life. Then they could have raised their vibration out of a state of wellbeing, and they could have manifested the type of relationship and the house that they wanted into their experience.

Again, it is all a matter of perspective, and what is important to one person may not be important at all to another. It is how you are deciding to look at the situation, and what you choose to believe and focus your thoughts on that create the outcome. It is a choice and you can shift your thoughts and beliefs.

If you are not able to shift your way of thinking about something that doesn't feel good, then shift your thoughts to something different that does feel good. This will help to remove resistance in your energetic vibration, and that will help in all areas. Sometimes there are situations that are very emotionally charged, and you may not see a way to shift your way of thinking to see it as a positive situation, although it is always possible. You can focus on something that you are grateful for in your life, or focus on what you would like to have in your life, or how you would like to see a situation resolved, or anything else that feels good, even if it is completely unrelated to the problem.

You would need to be focused to have an awareness of those lower vibrational thoughts as they came up, and intentionally shift them to something else. Once the resistance is removed, then your vibration rises, and you are back in alignment with your higher self, which is your natural state. It is only our own thoughts and beliefs that block us from being aligned with our true selves. Once in alignment, then you are at a much better starting point to attract everything you desire into your experience.

LET GO OF LIMITING BELIEFS

It may be necessary to let go of limiting beliefs. As an example, there were times in my life, that I didn't think it would be possible for me to have a loving relationship. I didn't have very good male role models, and my experiences with men were not very positive. There was a time that I didn't believe that there were good men out there. I was expecting the negative, so that is what I was drawing to myself. I didn't feel that I was lovable or that I had enough to offer someone wonderful due to the beliefs that I had about myself. I had to shift my beliefs in order to open myself up to a loving relationship.

There are people who don't believe that they are worthy of having a wonderful life and everything that goes along with that. That would be a very limiting belief. Another example would be that many people may feel like they are not capable of achieving what they want in life, so they don't even try, and they hold onto jobs or relationships that are unhealthy for them.

Becoming aware of what your beliefs are is very important in this introspective work. Many of these beliefs come from outside sources, family, friends, co-workers, organized religion, political leaders, and society in general. They do also come up from your own thoughts and perspectives on life. Your beliefs affect your thoughts, which create your emotions and behaviors, and ultimately what you are creating in your experience of physical reality. Really dig deep into understanding what your beliefs are. They also help you to determine how you identify yourself as a person.

A situation does not have a positive or negative meaning to it, until you create it with your thoughts, and your thoughts can be changed and then beliefs can be shifted. Even if you believe something is negative and can't see it in any other way, know that it is always possible to look at any situation in a positive way and remain in a positive state of being.

You can learn from an experience that you may have initially perceived as negative and focus on what you learned that will help you as you move forward in life. You can experience something that you do not prefer, and then be grateful for the experience that is showing you through the contrast of what you do not want, and is giving you a clearer understanding of what you do desire, so that you can then bring that preferred experience into your reality.

Many people may believe that when things fall apart, it is a bad experience, and while it may be difficult at the time, that perception can lead to an outcome that you may not prefer. I know from personal experience, when I lost a relationship and my job and felt my life was falling apart, I just trusted that it would open me up to much better things to come, and it did. It is all a choice in how you decide to look at something.

It is important to maintain a state of wellbeing and a positive outlook no matter what happens in order to receive a positive outcome. That is where your power is in creating a preferred reality.

Look deeply at the beliefs about yourself, who you are as a person, what you believe you are capable of, what you believe are your strengths and weaknesses, what is important to you, what you want to experience in life, how you view other people, and what you believe in general. As you become aware of your beliefs, then pay attention to your emotions, as they are indicators of being in or out of alignment with your true self. If a belief is out of alignment with your soul self, then try to look at it in a different way. Determine what belief you would need to have to create a preferred outcome. Once you can shift the belief, it will no longer be able to create a negative experience for you.

If you have a thought of what you want in life, but believe something is not possible, take a look at that belief as well. If something you desire is coming up in your thoughts, that means that it already exists in the field. You are able to see the option, because it is one of the potentials for you to tap into, based on your current energetic vibration. As your energetic vibration raises, you will be able to tap into more higher vibrational potentials.

You are not actually creating or manifesting anything, as everything already exists energetically. You are just tapping into those things that you are a vibrational match for that exist in the field, though your consciousness, and then you can create or manifest them into your physical experience. Every potential already exists. It's already done, you just have to remove the resistance to allow it into your physical experience.

If you decide to believe that what you want to experience is not possible, then you will bring a different experience into your reality, even if it is not what you prefer. It is that belief that will hold you back, and that belief can be changed. You are the one that decides what you believe.

We all have our own way of thinking about things, and for most people this has been their way of thinking for their entire lives. Be gentle with yourselves as you move through this process. It can take time to change those beliefs and thoughts that are holding you back from your highest potential, but it will be life changing.

If you exist, you are worthy of everything you desire in life. You are a spark of the creative source, which is perfect. It is only your beliefs and thoughts that hold you back from who you truly are and all you are capable of creating into your experience.

FOCUS ON THE HIGHER VIBRATION END OF THE SPECTRUM

This was brought up earlier regarding raising your vibration, but is very important to look at in the process of letting go as well.

We live in a world of polarities. Both sides of polar opposites, are really the same thing, but in different degrees. There isn't really a tipping point. I'll reference the example of temperature again. One side of the scale is cold and the other is hot. They are both just varying degrees of the same thing. There isn't a set line of where cold stops and hot begins. It is all a matter of perspective. It is the same with all things, low to high, or dark to light, etc.

If you focus your attention to the more positive and higher vibration side of the spectrum, then you will be able to let go of the focus on the lower vibrational side. If you focus on what you would like to achieve, then you will attract more of what you want. For example, if you want to let go of anxiety, focus your energy on bringing in more peace. If you want to let go of a past relationship, focus your energy on bringing in a new loving relationship that fulfills your desires. If you want to let go of financial problems, focus your attention on gaining prosperity.

LET GO OF FEAR

I am going to again reference a previous example used of when I was younger, and I had some very serious financial issues, even though I was working a lot. I wasn't making much money, and because of working irregular hours, my childcare expenses were very high. Because I was always in fear and was focusing on never having enough money, I kept myself in that situation. When I was able to accept the fact that being in fear and worrying were not helping and were only making things worse, I was able to accept the current situation. I accepted that I could only do the best that I could for any situation that came up.

Worry is a form of reverse manifestation. I let go of the fear and the belief that I was stuck in this situation, and

149

focused my attention on things getting better, and then they did.

People fear change, so despite the fact that they may know that they need to let go of a person or situation for their wellbeing, the fear of change keeps many people stuck in situations that are not good for them. Don't allow fear to hold you back.

Even though someone may not be happy in their job, or a relationship, or whatever the situation may be, there is a familiarity to it. Many people have a fear of the unknown. There are those that would rather stay in an abusive relationship due to the fear of being alone. If they could let go of the fear and come to a place of acceptance that there isn't anything wrong with being single, they would be much happier. It can actually be quite enjoyable not having to deal with anyone else, and it can be very liberating. Once you know you are in control of your reality, then there is nothing to fear.

Fear is energy that is being filtered through a negative belief that is not in alignment with your true self, and you can feel that energy within the body. Joy is an energy that is filtered through a belief that is in alignment with your higher self. So when you start feel that feeling of fear, that is when you should determine what belief is causing that fear, and look to make a shift in your way of thinking.

A technique to help in releasing fear is to become aware of that physical feeling within the body. This may feel like a ball of energy within the stomach area for many people.

Once you have that awareness, then detach the cause from it, so that feeling is no longer connected with a belief. It is just energy. Take some deep breaths, and with your intention just allow that energy to release from that uncomfortable feeling. Become aware of what belief you would need to have that would alleviate that feeling of fear. You can work with your intention to move that energy that is now neutral into that different belief system, or you can release it all together.

EVERYTHING IS RELATIVE

Perspective may also play a part in how you view things. Remember everything is relative. I will give you another example from my time of working as a product manager. I was in a meeting with a factory owner, and they were encouraging me to make an investment, not relating to our business, but they were just trying to be helpful. I mentioned that I didn't have the money to invest. Then they suggested just investing just a very small amount, like a few thousand dollars, like it was nothing. For me, at that time, that might as well have been all of the money in the world.

Always keep in mind that everything is relative. Someone who lives a mansion may feel that those who are living in a one-bedroom apartment are living in poverty and could not imagine that circumstance for themselves. However, there are many people in the world who are homeless or living in hut without water or electricity who may feel that the luxury of living in a one-bedroom apartment was out of their reach. One person's idea of poverty may be someone else's abundance, and just know that those thoughts or beliefs are choices that can be adjusted.

I used economic perspectives as an example, but seeing how differently people view the same things would help to see other options available for any belief system. Once we have an awareness of what our beliefs are, then we can start to look at situations from different perspectives to open ourselves to thinking about things differently.

ACCEPTANCE OR CHANGE

It is also important to surrender and go with the flow. Many people struggle and fight against the current. Not only do you not get to where you want to go, but you are stressed in the fighting.

Let go of trying to control the outcome of everything, especially that which you have no control over. Many people have it set in their mind that things need to be a certain way. The brain and logical mind are not meant to determine what you need to experience. The brain only allows for the experience itself. The higher mind is what you should be allowing to lead you to the experiences for your highest potential.

Acceptance is very important. Many people have difficulties in accepting some circumstances, and resist against them. Know that if you can't change a situation, all you can do is accept it or remove yourself from it.

Unfortunately, many people in situations that they cannot accept and are not going to change are not willing to make those changes themselves, so they allow themselves to remain in circumstances that they are not happy in and are having negative impacts on their lives. An example is someone that I did a reading for that was in a relationship with a married man. He had no intention of leaving his family for another woman. The other woman was in a relationship that she was not happy in for many different reasons. She wasn't willing to come to a place of acceptance of what the situation was, and she wasn't willing to let go of the situation either, so she was in a place of not being happy at all.

What she could have done is decided that because of the experience in this relationship, that she now knows that she wants a different type of relationship. She may prefer a partnership where she is not the last priority, and they can share experiences together in public, and not have to deal with a partners very limited available time for her. She could have let go of the relationship that she was never going to be happy with, but include some of the qualities of that relationship that she was happy with in her vision of a type of relationship that she would prefer. Then let go and allow her higher self to guide her to connect with the right person to open herself up to a loving relationship that she would have been happy with.

If you can't come to a place of acceptance and you are not willing to make a change, then you are accepting that you will never be happy. Many people do this with their jobs as well, but there are so many things that people hold onto that they cannot accept as they are and be happy with them.

If you are in a situation that you cannot accept for what it is, then focus your attention on what you would like to have for your life. Remember, you can look at this situation as an opportunity to let you know what you prefer, and then you can create a better experience for yourself.

You may have to let go of what you are not happy with and make your way to something different. Allow yourself to trust your inner guidance system to lead you to it. If you are insisting that something has to be different than it is, and you are holding on to it, that is a form of resistance. If it is something that is causing emotions that are not of joy and happiness, then that is your indication that this situation is not in alignment with your soul self.

You cannot reject or push against the unwanted and create what you want. When you are focused on the problem, you cannot find the solution. The solution is never where the problem is. The key is to shift your focus, and shift your thoughts away from the problem and to what you want to achieve. If it's not making you happy, and you are focusing your attention on what is making you unhappy, sad, angry, jealous, or any other lower vibrational emotion, then that is what you are continuing to manifest into your experience.

Many people have it set in their mind that things have to be a certain way. Then they are setting themselves up to not be happy, especially if what they want is not possible because there are other people involved or a situation cannot be changed. You cannot control anyone else in any situation. It doesn't matter what the situation is, you are only in control of your response and the choices that you make regarding the situation.

Happiness can't be conditional. If you will only be happy once you have what you want, then it will be difficult to attract that experience. You need to be in a place of wellbeing first, then those experiences that reflect that state of happiness will manifest in your life. Remember, the mirror will not smile back unless you are smiling first.

It is important to be able to let go of the insistence of what the logical brain is telling you must happen in order for you to be happy, and let go and go with the flow and trust your inner guidance system to take you where you need to go. Your logical brain only knows what it is experiencing, and your higher mind has the perspective of knowing all of the wonderful potentials that available for you. Your higher mind can guide you to experiences far greater than the logical mind can even think of. Let go of the resistance and the insistence and allow your higher mind to lead you to everything you desire in life.

LISTEN TO YOUR INTUITION

Your intuition is the higher dimensional part of yourself trying to guide you to what is best for your highest good. Unfortunately, many people do not listen to it, and are afraid of letting go. Or sometimes, people can't get beyond what logically makes sense, and they allow their logical mind to override the intuition. Remember that sometimes things need to end, in order to open you up to much better things. Your intuition will never lead you in the wrong direction. Once you learn to trust it, you will realize it is always accurate, and it will guide you to what is best for you.

You don't have to start with huge life changing decisions. Take baby steps with small decisions. Once you start to realize that you can trust your intuition, then you can use it to make larger decisions. It is like a muscle that can be strengthened with use. The more you trust your intuition, the stronger it will become.

Become more aware with how you receive this guidance from your higher self so that it is easier for you to recognize. It can be subtle, and it may not be received the same way for everyone. It can be that small voice inside, or a sense of knowing, or a vision, or a feeling

If you find yourself overthinking, then you are not trusting this guidance. Know that you can trust your intuition. It is communication from your soul self that has access to unlimited knowledge and a clear understanding of the highest potentials that are available for you to experience.

EXPRESS YOURSELF

Sometimes people hold things in, and it can help to release it through expressing yourself verbally or by writing down your thoughts. You can even burn the written intentions of what you need to release down, to show symbolically you are ready to let them go. It can be quite powerful.

FORGIVE

Forgive everything and everyone, even if the other person was wrong. We have all been hurt or wronged by others. It is important to forgive, not for others, but for yourself. That doesn't mean you are ok with what has been done or that you want to allow the other person to remain in your life. It just means that you are not going to allow them or what happened to have a negative effect on you anymore. You are letting go of any negative feelings that you are holding onto, that are only hurting yourself.

It is also important to forgive yourself for anything that you may regret as well. Holding onto regret does not change any situation for the better, but it will lower your energetic vibration. Learn from past experiences, but do not dwell on them. Move forward becoming who you are deciding to be in the future.

VISUALIZE WHAT YOU WANT TO LET GO OF

Another technique to help in letting go is to visualize releasing what you are ready to let go of. You can use your imagination to envision a vortex of white light moving through and around your body, and just pulling out all lower vibrational energies, which you may see as a grey energy, and moving them into the light to be transformed. Or you can see the white light moving from the top of your head through your body, moving all lower vibrational energies into the center of the Earth to be transformed. You can visualize the chakras becoming more open, brighter, spinning faster, and energy flowing through the body more freely. You can even do this while taking a shower, and visualize energy washing over you as you are under the water. It doesn't matter how you choose to visualize it. It is your intention that is the key.

SUMMARY OF KEY #2:
RAISING YOUR ENERGETIC VIBRATION

- Your energetic vibration affects your overall wellbeing in all areas mentally, emotionally, spiritually, and physically.

- Your natural state is of the highest vibration and is in alignment with your higher self. It is a state of peace, love, and joy.

- Lower vibrational thoughts and emotions cause resistance and reduce the flow of energy, lowering the energetic vibration.

- You attract experiences that you are a vibrational match to into your physical reality.

- Some techniques that will help in raising your energetic vibration include: meditation, feeling joy, connecting with nature, gratitude and appreciation, spending less time with electronics, mindfulness, gentle movements, eating healthy, opening the heart, working with crystals, sound vibration, and energy healing.

- The most important way to increase the energetic vibration is through introspection and letting go of lower vibrational thoughts and beliefs that cause energetic resistance and block the flow of energy.

- Emotions are the indicators of your energetic vibration. Any lower vibrational emotion such as: sadness, guilt, fear, worry, stress, anger, anxiety, etc. are indicating a thought or belief that is not in alignment with your higher self.

- Higher vibrational emotions such as excitement, joy, and love are indications that you are in alignment.

- There are 7 main chakras, which are energetic centers that are the receiving and transmitting points of energy within the physical body. The energetic vibration is determined on the flow of energy though the chakras.

- Lower vibrational emotions cause a reduction or a slowing of the flow of energy through the chakras. This creates an energetic resistance which limits the access to the higher self and other higher dimensional energies.

- Each chakra connects to different areas of emotions related to our physical experience.

- It is not necessary to connect the lower vibrational emotion, thought, belief, or behavior to a specific chakra in order to do the work to let go of what is holding you back, but it is important to work through those things through

160

introspection of them.

- Some techniques to work with specifically for chakra balance include: working with your intention and visualization, utilizing specific crystals and other tools, color or sound vibrations corresponding to the chakras, using affirmations, and energy healing.

- The most important part is the introspective work in understanding what you are holding on to that is limiting your energetic vibration and looking at what thoughts and beliefs are the cause, and then shifting or letting go of them.

- Techniques to utilize in letting go of lower vibrational thoughts and emotions include: working with your intention, stop living in the past, shifting your thoughts, letting go of limiting beliefs, focus on the higher vibrational side of the spectrum, let go of fear, view things from a different perspective, know that to maintain a sense of wellbeing you can either accept a situation or make a change, listen to your intuition, express yourself, forgive everyone including yourself, and visualize what you want to let go of.

- Know that you are in control of your energetic vibration. There is not any other person or situation that can have any effect on you or what you experience in life, unless you allow it.

- You are the only one that is responsible for your energy through your thoughts, beliefs, emotions, and behaviors, and therefore you are in total control of your creating your experience in life.

- The key to creating an experience you prefer is to master the mind and consciously create. Otherwise you are just experiencing what you have created as a result of the chaos of random thoughts and emotions, which in most cases will lead you to a reality that you do not prefer.

Key #3:
Consciously Creating All You Desire

WHAT IS IT THAT YOU DESIRE TO EXPERIENCE?

Now that you have an understanding of who you are as a multi-dimensional being, understand how energy and the Universe works, know about the importance of your energetic vibration and know how to raise your vibration to the highest level possible, it is time to consciously manifest the experiences that you prefer into your reality.

You are not manifesting anything out of nothing. Everything already exists. If you can think it, it is already there in the field energetically as a potential. All you have to do is make sure that you are have released any energetic resistance so that you are a vibrational match and then you can tap into it though your consciousness with your thoughts and intentions, and then you will bring the experience into your physical reality.

This is not just a theory or something that is a suggestion on what may work. This is how your physical experience is created. What you experience is a reflection of your

164

consciousness, and you have the ability to control that.

Also, there is a perception that when you are manifesting, you are energetically bringing what you want to experience from someplace else. The field or what some call the vortex is not a location that is outside of yourself. Everything is right here. Every part of the energy field that is All That Is contains the whole, and that is the divine oneness that we are all a part of. Every particle in both energetic and physical existence is here and now.

You can create a life you desire! I know from personal experience. I went from living in poverty, nearly being homeless, feeling alone and unloved, and working in jobs that I did not like to taking control of my experience and now I am in a financial position where I'm not worried about money, I have lots of love in my life, a very happy marriage, I'm able to travel the world and experience everything I ever desired, I have a beautiful metaphysical store and healing studio that I love and is helping others at the same time. I can look back at anything that I've put the energy into creating in my life, I have achieved. This is a never-ending process, as there is always room for more wonderful things to experience in life.

Unfortunately, most people just don't realize that they can consciously create the life of their dreams, and they fall victim to the chaos of random thoughts and emotions that are in reaction to what they are experiencing. If you are focused on what you are currently experiencing, then it isn't likely that you are going to experience anything that is very different. Unless, you are also adding fear, worry, or any other lower vibrational thought or emotion into that situation, and then you may create something worse.

What we are currently experiencing was created from old energy, past thoughts and beliefs. You are creating your future experience from the present moment and you are in control of your thoughts and beliefs at this moment. You don't have to go down the same path if you want to create something different.

We are all creating our reality, whether we are doing it consciously or unconsciously. It is happening unconsciously as a response with your uncontrolled thoughts and emotions, or intentionally as a creation, but you are deciding your reality either way.

It is easy to get caught up in life, and just react to what you see happening in front of you. There are the distractions of work, bills, laundry, chores, and everything else that needs to be done that can take your attention away from consciously creating what you want in life.

The first step in manifesting what you want to experience, is to know what you want. Now this seems obvious, but most people are so busy just living their lives day to day, and just responding to what they are experiencing, that there may not be a lot of thought or focus on what they want in life. Even when there is focus on what they want, it can be because of an awareness of what they don't want and that is really where their focus is, on what they are not happy with. There are also some people that spend their lives sitting in front of the TV, and just exist, without any thought of bringing anything better into their lives.

Take some time and really think about what it is that you want in life. Write it down. That will help bring you clarity and it is also bringing it into the physical realm. Don't limit yourself, think big. Your only limitation is by your own thoughts and beliefs, and you are in control of those. This can be anything from better finances, relationships, career opportunities, travel, a new home or any other material object, better health, joy, peace, spiritual enlightenment, or anything else.

There are no limitations on what you can create, anything is possible as long as you truly believe that you can, and you are able to focus and master your thoughts, emotions, and intentions, and listen to your intuition and take inspired action to lead you to what you wanted to create. Know your power!

There is room to write in this book. You may need additional paper or a notebook. Don't limit yourself to what there is room to write down. It can be very powerful to go back months and years later and look at what you were successful in bringing into your life. In areas that you were not successful in manifesting what you desire into your experience, you can do a little more introspective work to understand why, and then you can make changes from there.

WHAT I DESIRE TO BRING INTO MY LIFE:

HOW TO MANIFEST EVERYTHING YOU DESIRE

As you are now aware, the higher your energetic vibration, the better it is for your overall wellness in all areas (mental, emotional, physical, and spiritual). The higher your vibration, the easier it is to consciously create as well. There is a better flow of energy to not hold anything back. Any lower vibrations you are holding onto within your body creates resistance and slows down the manifestation process. We have already gone through the importance of this and how to raise your vibration in the last section, so we won't go into too much detail again, but this is just another reminder in how it relates specifically to creating everything you desire into your life.

There are several different techniques that you can use to create everything you desire in your life. Utilize what resonates with you. The more of these you can try, the better.

KNOW YOUR POWER AS A MULTI-DIMENSIONAL BEING

When you know that you are much more than what you experience in this material world, you can connect to the higher dimensional parts of yourself to create anything you want in your life. You can utilize that part of yourself that has access to unlimited knowledge, is not limited by space and time, and will guide you to your highest potential.

The more that you can identify with yourself as a soul, the easier it is to break away from the limitations created by the ego, personality, habits, excuses, environments, and other people's thoughts and expectations.

Even though we are living in a three-dimensional world, we are also connected to higher dimensions, and we can work with those higher dimensional energies. They may not be visible to us, but they do exist. Our thoughts and emotions are also higher dimensional energies, and we can utilize them to create.

UNDERSTANDING THE LAW OF ATTRACTION

This was brought up in the first section of the book in understanding how the Universe works, but it is very important in manifestation. Our thoughts, feelings, words, intentions, and actions affect our energetic vibration, which will attract people, things, and experiences that are a vibrational match. Your energy is like a magnet. What you send out in the form of energy is what you will attract back to yourself. This can be good or bad, depending on what you are putting out to the Universe through your thoughts and emotions.

It is necessary to shift your thoughts to what you want to create, and not focus on what is lacking or what you are not happy with. In difficult times, it is easy to focus on the problem, but in order to bring a positive change, it is necessary to focus on the solution or the desired outcome.

You first need to be aware of your thoughts and feelings. This sounds obvious, but most people are just going through their daily activities, and they don't have a very good awareness.

Once you have the awareness, then you need to shift your lower vibrational thoughts immediately to focus on the higher vibrational side of what you are desiring to achieve. As an example, if you want to find love, you can't focus on the sadness or disappointment of not having anyone in your life currently. You need to focus on what you want to bring into your experience. The moment you start to think about what you are not happy about, shift your thoughts to what you want to bring into your life. It takes the same amount of time and energy to imagine wonderful possibilities as it does to focus on what you are not happy about, but the results are very different.

The Universe doesn't speak in English or any other language, it understands vibration only. Your thoughts are energies, but it is the energy behind the words of your thoughts that really count. For example, if you are not happy with your current job, and your thoughts are "I want a new career", but you are regularly focused on what you are frustrated with in your current job, then it is the vibration matching your frustration and being unhappy at work that will create the experience of staying in that unwanted situation. You need to be very aware of what the energy is beyond what the words are stating.

Remember that the vibration of "wanting" is very different than that of "having" or "experiencing". The state of wanting can bring increased awareness that you do not have what you desire. It can hold you in that place of continuing to want something, rather than actually experiencing it.

You can create the vibration of "having" or "experiencing" through your thoughts about what you desire, in placing yourself in that experience as if it is already happening through your imagination. Then that creates emotions that will be a vibrational match to that experience.

You also don't want to be disappointed if it isn't happening soon enough, or to be focused on asking "Why don't I have this yet?", or "Why hasn't this manifested?". That is bringing your attention back to the fact that you do not have what you want, and it will hold you in the state of not having what you desire.

It is important to maintain a positive state of being, no matter what happens. That is the way to create a positive outcome. Trust that what happens is for a reason, even if it isn't what you wanted. It may be to help guide you to something better or for a lesson to learn that will help you as you move forward. Go with the flow of what is happening, and trust that your higher self will guide you to what is best for you through your intuition, the feeling of joy, and synchronicity.

Your emotions are the indicator of where your vibration is at, and they will let you know where work needs to be done in shifting the thoughts or beliefs that are causing energetic resistance. If you think about something you want and do not feel good about it, because you don't have it yet or you don't think that you can achieve it, then that is an indication that you are not in alignment with what you desire.

You can shift the vibration by shifting your thoughts or beliefs about the current situation until there is no longer the resistance. If that is not possible, then you can shift your thoughts to what you want to achieve until you are at a place where you can think about whatever you would like to change and feel good about it.

CAUSE AND EFFECT

Every intention sets energy in motion. The "field" of potentials for you to experience is constantly changing based on your shifting thoughts, emotions, intentions, and actions. What you send out through your thoughts, emotions, and intentions are a cause of what results in your reality. If you are sending intentions of love, compassion, kindness, respect, integrity, etc., you will receive more of those in your life as well as a result.

I'm sure you are aware of the common saying "you reap what you sow". This is another way of stating that you receive into your physical life what you send out energetically.

Your life is a reflection of your consciousness. If you are looking at a mirror, you can't expect the mirror to smile back at you if you are not smiling first. Physical reality will only show you a reflection based on your vibration. You can't decide I will be happy, once whatever it is you want happens, and expect the mirror of life to give you that reflection before you make the changes you need to make first. You would need to be happy first, and then your reality will show you the reflection with those experiences that support that state of wellbeing.

What you experience in life is a direct result of your thoughts, beliefs, behaviors, and actions. What you put out is what you attract back. It is important to understand this so that you can energetically send out more of what is in alignment of what you want to receive back in your life.

IS WHAT YOU WANT IN ALIGNMENT WITH YOUR SOUL?

It is important to know if what you want to bring into your life is best for you on a soul level. Does it connect with your soul truth? An example that I have previously noted is the time that I was working in the apparel industry as a senior product manager. When I started, I was the only one in the department, and over the years it had grown substantially. There was an opening for a director position that I wanted, and I felt should have been offered to me, as I had put my heart and soul into that job, not to mention a lot of long hours and hard work. However, that wasn't what I truly wanted at a soul level, that was coming from my ego and my logical mind. It was never going to make me happy or fulfilled. I felt that I deserved it, but it was never what was best for me at a soul level.

Another example would be wanting to move forward in a relationship for the wrong reasons. If you wanted to move forward in a relationship that was never going to truly make you happy because you didn't want to be alone or because you wanted security, that would be another example of something you may have thought that you wanted, but wasn't your soul truth of wanting what is best for you. You can tell if it is your soul's truth of what you truly want by utilizing your intuition and how it makes you feel. It will feel good if it is in alignment with your true self.

Many also people allow themselves to be guided based on other people's expectations or out of fear of what others will think. Family can be a big influence. Others will allow themselves to be influenced by advice from friends, co-workers, religious leaders, or others. Other people may mean well in trying to direct you, but you are the only one that has access to the guidance system that your soul self provides. What may be good for them, may not be a good path for you. Also, other people may try to hold you back out of their own sense of worry, fear, or concern for your wellbeing. They may mean well, but if you aren't following your own path, it can keep you from manifesting what is best for yourself at a soul level.

Your higher self knows what you came into this life to accomplish and learn from, and also has an awareness of what are the highest potentials available for you in in the field, and it can utilize all of the knowledge in the Universe. Utilize your own inner guidance system to lead you to everything you desire in life.

LISTEN TO YOUR INTUITION

This is very important. So many people know intuitively what is best for them, but then allow their logical mind to distract them from the guidance leading them in the right direction. Also, many people allow fear to keep them from making changes or taking action on what they are intuitively being guided to.

Really pay attention to that feeling in your heart. The more you realize what it feels like to receive intuitive information and act on it, the more you will be able to count on it. What is best for you at a soul level, may not be the logical option, but your intuition can guide you to everything you desire.

As an example, when I quit my job to open The Sacred Journey, that was definitely not what made sense logically. At the time, my income was supporting my family. I wasn't happy in my current job and working for others anymore, and I trusted my intuition, and I've never been happier in my life. Once I took some steps forward in deciding what I wanted, synchronicities happened to help create the reality. When I first had the thought of what I wanted to do, there wasn't any money saved for that, so it was strange to even be thinking about opening a store. Out of nowhere I received a call from a lawyer that wanted to come to an agreement for a payout for past due child support from my ex, starting from more than twenty years prior. That provided exactly the amount needed to open the store. Then after I quit my job, they asked me to continue working for them, doing my same job, but with less hours put in and only a couple of partial days in the office. This allowed us to survive and continue to put money in to grow our business. I had to take the leap of faith first, and then everything came together perfectly. We were also guided to the best sources for product and to people that we still have great business relationships with today.

I trust my intuition completely. I know that I will be guided to what I need that is in my best interest. Remember, your brain and logical mind are limited by your physical experience. They are not what should be guiding you. Your higher mind has access to everything you desire, unlimited knowledge, your life plan, all of your highest potentials, and knows how to work with synchronicity so everything falls in to place perfectly.

It is so scary for people to let go of living from their logical mind and trust their intuition. Realize that your intuition is the way your soul communicates to you. You can trust it.

COME FROM A PLACE OF LOVE

It is important to create from a place of love, and not fear. Listen to your heart. If you are coming from a place of love, that is going to give you some momentum in the creation process.

As an example, if you want to create better health, you don't want to come from a place of fear about a health condition. You want to come from a place of self-love and wanting to create a better state of health for yourself.

Fear creates resistance, and love creates momentum.

TRUST IS A POWERFUL FORCE

When you have trust that you can manifest everything you want, that helps with the momentum of bringing what you desire into your reality. You are letting go of the resistance and allowing yourself into the flow. It is important to not move through the resistance of doubt, fear, stress, or worry.

This is difficult for many people. It's ok if you take baby steps. Don't jump off a cliff if you don't know you will fly, and don't quit your job unless you trust in the Universe to provide everything you need. Start with something small, utilizing everything that you now know. Once you start to see that you really are in control of what you are experiencing in your life, then you will feel more comfortable with taking bigger steps.

CLARITY IS IMPORTANT

When you have decided on what you want to manifest, it is important to be very clear on as many details as possible. The more clearly that you know what you want, the more likely it is that you will create what you will be most happy with. Then you can visualize it easier as well.

Make a clear choice. If you are indecisive or uncertain, it blocks the flow of energy. Once you have made a clear decision, then opportunities will open up.

FOCUS ON WHAT YOU DESIRE, NOT HOW TO GET IT

You don't need to have all of the details of how to get to what you want, and that will allow the Universe to open up the path of least resistance to get you to your goal. Many people think it is necessary to manifest money to get you to what you really want, but that isn't always necessarily the case. Be open to any paths that open up. As an example, our trip to Costa Rica was something I wanted to manifest. I listened to my intuition and created the retreat through the store. Because we brought other people with us, our trip didn't cost us anything. It also opened an opportunity to help other people that benefited from the experience as well.

It can be helpful to focus on what you desire at the core level. Many people feel that they desire more money, but they may really desire the feeling of peace of mind that comes with not having to worry about finances and the knowing that all of their needs are met. It can be helpful to focus on that feeling that you want to create, rather than focusing on manifesting the money. Financial abundance may be the path of least resistance that brings you what you desire, but it may come in another form that you don't want to block by having the insistence that it is the only way.

Once you know what you want, and you have enough detail about it to feel the excitement about it, as if it has already happened, then let go of the insistence of exactly how it has to happen and every detail about it. Trust that your higher mind can figure it out much better than your logical mind can. It can bring you something even better than you ever could imagine, once you let go of the insistence that it has to be exactly as you envision, and that it has to be obtained through the path to get there that your logical mind has created.

FOLLOW YOUR JOY

In any situation, if you follow the option that brings you the strongest feeling of joy or excitement, without fear, you will be headed towards the path for your highest good.

That feeling of joy or excitement that you feel at your heart center is how your higher self is communicating to you. It doesn't speak to you in words, it comes through a feeling. That feeling is what is guiding you through life. Follow it.

The feeling of joy is your true nature. You feel joy when you are in alignment with your higher self. It is only the resistance of lower vibrational beliefs, thoughts, and emotions that block that feeling. However, when you are not feeling peace, joy, and love, then you can still look at it in a positive way because it is indicating to you that there is something holding you back, and then you can do the introspective work to determine what belief or thought is causing the resistance in your vibration. Then you can shift accordingly to become back in alignment with your true self.

Unfortunately, many people disregard that feeling of joy or excitement, and move through life with what is safe or logically makes sense. Other people may listen initially, but then allow fear or negative thinking to change their path, by those thoughts and emotions changing the strongest potentials in the field.

If you continually use that feeling of joy or excitement to lead you, it can be a roadmap to guide you to what you want to experience in life. Even if it isn't a direct link to what you are trying to manifest, it can lead you to the right person, circumstance, or information that can lead you closer to what you want to achieve. It may even be leading you to an experience that will help to increase your energetic vibration, which will allow for easier manifestation.

FEEL THE PASSION

Emotion is a higher dimensional energy that helps bring forward everything you want to create. Emotion is energy in motion. When you think about what you want, really feel the emotion you will feel, as if it has already manifested. Emotion is another powerful force that will help you to manifest.

It is important to feel that feeling of having or experiencing what you desire, because that feeling is what will match the vibration of what you want to manifest. The vibration and feeling of wanting something is very different than the feeling of experiencing or having it, even if you are still in the process of manifesting and haven't actually brought it into your reality yet. You can still feel the emotion of it as if it has already happened though your thoughts about it.

If there is something that I want to create, I can feel what I would feel if I were experiencing what I wanted to manifest. I do this with vacation planning a lot, which is one of my favorite things to manifest. Even at times when I didn't have very much money, I would plan vacations as if it were going to happen. I knew where I wanted to go, what hotels I would stay at, and what activities I would do while there. I would look at photos and read other travelers reviews, so I could imagine the experience clearly. I would feel the excitement of what the experience would be like, as if I were there already. I've been able to manifest the most amazing travel experiences, even when it didn't seem possible.

I've traveled all over the world, with trips to Costa Rica, Mexico City, and Egypt in just the last year. I currently have trips to Turkey, The Galapagos and Ecuador, and Thailand and Cambodia in the planning stages. Just thinking about these trips makes me happy, and that feeling is drawing these experiences closer. I'm having fun and enjoying the process of the research and planning, and I am excited for the actual experiences that I know are coming soon.

VISUALIZE IT

When you visualize, you are creating an energetic imprint of what you want to manifest. You can see what you want to bring into your reality within your mind's eye, and then you are sending that energetically out to the field to tap into that potential and bring it into your reality. It also helps you to create the details that you want in the outcome.

Then be open to what may come to you through your intuition to make the experience even better than you could have imagined. Start with the knowing, then the clarity, and the vision, but then pay attention to what you are being guided to and be open to adjustments. Know that your higher self will guide you to what you desire or something even greater. If you are not flexible, and you insist it must be only one way, then you may be missing out on something even better. If you are insistent on there only being one way to get you to what you want to experience, then you may be closing off the path of least resistance to get you to what you desire, which could cause delays.

187

The key is to have trust and allow yourself to be guided by your higher self through your intuition and the feelings of joy or excitement. Know that whatever happens, there is a reason for it. Maintain a state of wellbeing no matter what happens. Even if it is something that you do not prefer, then it will give you clarity on what you do desire. It is possible to look at any situation in a positive way, and that is the only way to receive a positive outcome.

COMMUNICATION

It is helpful to be able to communicate exactly what you want to create. Communication is an exchange of energy and information. This may be communicating with other people that can work with you in this manifestation, or being able to communicate it to the higher dimensional energies (higher self, spirit guides, loved ones in spirit, angels) that can assist you with bringing what you want into your reality. You can even request for your higher self to communicate and work with the higher selves of others in order to help you to manifest a particular outcome.

GRATITUDE

Even though you are manifesting something that you do not yet have, it is very important to feel appreciation and gratitude for all that is good in your life. Feel gratitude for even the little things, like a beautiful sunset, a song you enjoy, or a delicious meal. The more feelings of gratitude you have, the easier it is to attract more things that will give you that same feeling of appreciation, because what you are sending out to the Universe in the form of energy is what you will attract back to yourself. Every time you feel appreciation for something, you are telling the Universe "more of this, please".

You can also feel gratitude for what is yet to come, having trust that all of the wonderful things you desire are on their way into your life.

SHIFTING THOUGHTS AND BELIEFS

We have already discussed the importance of this in raising your vibration and letting go of what is holding you back, but it is also very important in the manifestation process.

There are two sides to everything, a lower vibrational side and a higher vibrational side. We live in a world of polarity. Whether the view is positive or negative, beautiful or ugly, convenient or difficult depends totally on the mind and the chosen perspective.

Think of each of these opposites being on different sides of a stick. Hot/cold, or low/high, or good/bad, or anything else on opposite sides the stick. They are really all the same thing, but in varying degrees. There isn't a set mark of exactly when one side moves to the other. If your focus is on the lower vibrational side of it, that is what your consciousness is going to reflect back to you. If you have noticed yourself focusing on the lower vibrational side of any situation, you can shift your focus to what you would like to experience on the other side of the stick.

It is also important that you are not coming from a place of focusing on what is missing in your life or what you are not happy with. You need to be happy and in a place of acceptance of whatever place you are at in order to create something better. You cannot have negative thoughts, beliefs, or emotions, and create a positive experience.

You also want to be mindful of your thoughts and beliefs. If you are focused on what you desire to manifest in your life, but that little voice in your mind is saying "I can't do that", or "that isn't going to happen", or whatever else it may be telling you, that is going to cause resistance.

PRAYER

Prayer is the communication between our physical selves and the higher dimensional forces of light. It can be asking for guidance or direction that can help you to manifest what you want to bring into your life. It can be a communication to the Universe, to your higher self, to your loved ones in spirit, to your spirit guides, angels, or any other higher dimensional energy.

With that communication, you are also working with your intention of what you desire to bring into your life. You are focusing on what you want to manifest. You have a clear thought in order to be able to communicate it, even if it is a communication through your mind with the thoughts you are sending out energetically.

MEDITATION

In the practice of clearing your mind, you can potentially receive information, guidance, or clarity from higher dimensional energies. This may come through a message, vision, thought, feeling, or knowing.

You are also clearing your mind of all resistant thought, and this will help to raise your energetic vibration, which allows for easier manifesting.

Here is a meditation specifically created for manifestation. You may want to record yourself reading the meditation and play it back while you are in a relaxed state. Just as we have done with the last meditation in clearing the chakras, there will be room for some automatic writing to be done just after the meditation, so you may able to receive additional guidance from your higher self or other spiritual guides. While you are in that state of a higher vibration, it is easier to connect to higher dimensional energies. Since your vibration is higher, it is also a good time to set your intention of what you want to bring into your life.

At the end of the meditation, see what comes to you without any thought, just putting the pen to paper and seeing what comes though. Make sure that you have a pen and paper ready, so you don't have to go searching for one after the meditation. There is also space to write in this book after the meditation, so you can review this information that came through for you at a later time as well.

Close your eyes and take a deep breath. Just take some time to be present in this moment and become aware of every breath in and every breath out. Breathe in slowly and deeply. Breathing down into the diaphragm, you should feel your stomach move out as you breathe in and fill the lungs with air. Then releasing the air from your lungs as you slowly breath out. Take several deep breaths.

Relax your body. Become aware of any tension you feel in your body and allow your muscles to relax and feel loose.

Clear your mind as best as possible. If a thought comes in, just allow it to flow out, and then go back to focusing on your breathing. Just breathe, and just be.

Take a moment and think of what it is that you want to bring into your life. There may be many, but at this time, focus on only one. What is it that you most want to bring into your reality?

See this very clearly in your mind. Pay attention to all of the details. Use as many of your senses as possible. If this is something you can touch, pay attention to what it will feel like. If it is something that you will experience, see the vision of it happening in your mind, and notice all of the details of everything surrounding this experience. Whatever it is that you are manifesting, feel the emotion that you will feel when this comes into your life, as if you have already brought it into your reality.

Now visualize what you want to create as a ball of energy in the palm of your hands. Feel your connection to the higher dimensional part of yourself. Visualize and feel energy in the form of a beautiful bright white light pouring down from high in the universe over and though you, starting at the top of your head. This light is so bright it is almost blinding, think the color of lightning. It is iridescent, like a bubble in the sun, and sparkling. Feel it move through your crown chakra at the top of your head and move down into your heart center.

With this beautiful energy, focus on the feeling of how you will feel, once you have what you want most in life at this moment. The energy at your heart is expanding. Now see this energy and emotion moving through your arms and out the palms of your hands, and into the ball of light that is holding the ball of energy that is representing what you want to create. See this ball of light in the palm of your hands getting bigger and brighter. Now see this ball of light expand up into the universe. Know that this will come back to you in your reality, when the timing is best for your soul.

Align with your higher self. You may see this as a ball of iridescent bright white light, with a brighter light at the center. Allow this energy to merge with your physical body. The bright light in the center of this beautiful energy will align with the light at your heart center. You may feel like it clicks in place. Just breathe and feel this connection.

Ask for guidance regarding anything you need to know regarding what you desire to manifest or how to consciously create everything that you want to bring into your life.

When you are ready, slowly open your eyes. Without any thought, put your pen to the paper, and allow information to flow through you from your higher self. You may be surprised at the insights that you receive.

AUTOMATIC WRITING / MANIFESTATION

WORKING TOGETHER COLLECTIVELY

When you have multiple people working together for a particular outcome or experience, the energy created has even more power. My husband and I are very good at manifesting vacations, because we are always on the same page of what experience we want to bring into our lives. Because we are both manifesting the same experience, the energy is stronger.

This is also why we come together in groups at the store in our healing circles. Together we can have so much more of an impact than any one of us can have individually.

INSPIRED ACTION

When you work with energy to manifest something into your life, chances are it isn't just going to magically appear. There is usually some form of action that supports your desires that will need to take place. You may notice synchronicities appearing and your intuition guiding you to the next steps.

If you are wanting to manifest a new car that is not currently in your budget, chances are it isn't just going to magically appear in your driveway. You will have to take action. You would want to do some research. You may find a synchronicity in finding a great deal or possibly an opportunity to bring in more money to help you with the purchase. Then you would still need to move forward in taking action to make the purchase.

The energy that you are sending out will attract the things, people, experiences, circumstances, and opportunities that resonate with that same vibration. You can then listen to your intuition that will guide you to the next steps needed to bring in exactly what you were intending to manifest.

The action part is where some people get stuck. They can work energetically with their intentions, but then they hold back when it comes time to actually do the steps that it takes to get to what they want.

OVERCOME CHALLENGES

There may be challenges that come up as you try to manifest what you want. How you will succeed is dependent on how you view those challenges. You can look at them as roadblocks, or you can look at them as stepping stones to move through, or opportunities to create solutions. The key is to focus on finding the solution, rather than focusing on the problem.

CREATE A VISION BOARD

This is putting together images of what you want to bring into your life. This also helps you to see it clearly. You can keep these images in a place you will see them regularly to help to affirm that you are manifesting them into your life. You don't have to cut out pictures from magazines, you can find them online and put them onto a page, and print it out or maybe even set it as a screensaver or view it from time to time, when you are thinking about what you want to bring into your reality.

Remember to not be insistent that it needs to be exactly like the picture you have in mind. Be open in order to allow your higher self to guide you to something that may be even better for you. The image is just a place holder to allow for that energy of excitement about what you are manifesting to create the vibration you need to match that of what you want to experience in your life.

THE POWER OF "I AM" AFFIRMATIONS

Affirmations are very powerful, as they are acknowledging your own power of intention. Your intention is the most positive creative life force there is, and it is so much more powerful than most people realize.

It is especially powerful to use affirmations that start with "I am". This is for multiple reasons. First you are creating from the present moment. When you are stating with "I want" or "I will", what you desire is always going to be ahead of you, so it may not manifest, because you will always be "wanting" it or it "will" always be in the future. There is only "Now", and you can only create from the present.

Another reason that "I am" affirmations are so powerful is because you are connecting with the higher dimensional part of yourself. The word "I" is the ignition key of creation. What follows the word "I" turns the key and starts the engine of manifestation.

You are also very confidently stating what is. It is important to believe what you are putting out there to the Universe to have the full power of the energy behind the affirmation.

Many people have these "I am" thoughts and beliefs that identify who they are and their reality. These are not always positive, but you can consciously shift these statements to re-define the thoughts of who you are and what you are creating. If you are saying to yourself "I am not able to" or "I'm not good at", you are putting that negative affirmation into the collective consciousness. Shift those affirmations to what you want to create, and in knowing that you are in charge of the creation of your reality, you will shift your power to be and create everything you want.

Here is a wonderful example of a "I am" affirmation, but there are no limits: "I am consciously creating everything I desire in my life"

Speaking your intentions out loud or writing them down can also be beneficial. That is bringing them into your physical reality.

PUT YOUR INTENTION IN WATER

If you are familiar with Dr. Emoto's work, you are aware that water reacts to energy. Through scientific experiments he was able to prove that water crystals form beautiful patterns with positive thought, words, and intentions. The opposite happens with negative words. It isn't the words themselves that create the effect, it is the energy or vibration behind them.

You can fill a glass of water. Put your intention on a sticky note and attach it to the glass. There is power in writing your intentions down. Read it out loud. There is power in speaking affirmations as well. You can even visualize the energy of the intention going into the water in the form of energy. Then drink the water. The water that is energetically holding your intention goes into all of the cells in your body.

Your body is approximately 70% water. Knowing that intention, words, thoughts, and emotion affect the structure of the water accordingly, imagine how much of an effect you can have. You can utilize this method in manifestation of anything that you would like to desire, including physical healing.

You can also put your intention into the air you are breathing or the food you are eating as well.

PHYSICAL CONNECTIONS TO THE HIGHER SELF

Within your body is a connection to the higher dimensional part of yourself. You can access higher dimensional energy through the physical body by doing some resistance testing. If you are not certain about something, you can get additional clarity through your physical body. If you want to confirm what you want is the best path for you at a soul level, then you can check by holding your thumb and middle finger together. With your other hand, put your thumb and fingers below the contact point and to try to move them apart. You will notice for a "yes" answer, your fingers will move apart easily. Where there is resistance, your fingers will remain together or be difficult to move apart.

You can also use a pendulum as a tool to connect with your higher self to receive guidance regarding what you want to create or how to achieve the manifestation. You can ask the pendulum "What is the movement for yes?", and then "What is the movement for no?", and then you can ask "yes" or "no" questions and see how the pendulum moves for the answer. You can also use the pendulum with charts to point to letters, numbers, words, areas of the body, or any other information you may need.

The pendulum will also show how open your chakras are in relation to each other, so you can see where there may be energetic blockages if energy isn't flowing properly. Just ask to show the movement for each chakra, one by one, and notice where the pendulum moves faster or opens in comparison to the chakras where you may see it slow down or narrow. Once you are aware of areas that may need work in order to raise your energetic vibration, you can make those adjustments. Once your vibration is raised, you will be able to manifest what you desire more easily and quicker.

There are other divination tools that you can use to connect with your higher self and receive insight and guidance. You can use Tarot or oracle cards or message boards as a physical connection to receive guidance from your higher self.

CRYSTALS AND OTHER TOOLS

We have already talked about how crystals affect our energetic vibration, but they are also wonderful tools to use in the manifestation process.

They work together with your intention. Every time you see the crystal or pick it up to hold it or put it in your pocket, you are reminding yourself of your intention, which is speaking to the universe and tapping into what you want to bring into your life.

I always tell people who are shopping for crystals in our store to pay attention to what you are drawn to. In most cases your intuition will guide you to the crystal with the energy that is best for you at that moment. You can also pay attention to the properties, and select a crystal or crystals based off of what you would like to attract into your life.

There are different crystals that are used for different reasons, such as drawing in love, abundance, protection, joy, peace, or balance and chakra alignment. The crystals have different energies that help in particular areas. I have listed some crystals that have energies that will resonate with a particular purpose, but there are others as well. The key is to tap into what resonates with yourself.

Prosperity-
Citrine, Jade, Pyrite, Peridot, Aventurine, Tiger's Eye, Topaz, Moss Agate

Love-
Rose Quartz, Rhodonite, Rhodochrosite, Malachite, Aventurine, Emerald

Protection-
Black Tourmaline, Obsidian, Smokey Quartz, Malachite, Hematite, Jet

Spiritual Connection-
Clear Quartz, Selenite, Amethyst, Labradorite, Lapis Lazuli, Celestite, Sugilite, Angelite, Prehnite, Azurite

Peace and Tranquility-
Amethyst, Blue Calcite, Larimar, Rose Quartz, Moonstone, Mangano Calcite, Lepidolite, Blue Lace Agate, Howlite, Scolecite, Pink Opal, Aquamarine

World Peace Healing-
Shungite, Clear Quartz, Mangano Calcite, Rose Quartz, Smokey Quartz, Selenite, Sugilite, Chrysocolla

Happiness and Joy-
Sunstone, Citrine, Carnelian, Rose Quartz, Chrysoprase, Watermelon Tourmaline

There are many different ways to use crystals. I didn't even realize how many ways that I use them until I started writing them down for the class on crystals that I teach at our store. Here are some of the different options.

- Many crystals are stunningly beautiful. You may want to have them as decoration, so you can enjoy their beauty as well as their energy.

- You can hold them in your hand during meditation to work with their energy or work on the intention that you have for the crystal.

- You can carry the crystals with you in a bag in your pocket, or many women have kept them in their bra, so you can have them on you to receive the vibrational benefits from the crystal at all times.

- You can wear them in jewelry, which can be very beautiful, match to your outfit, and it is another way to receive the benefits from having the crystal near you all day.

- You can use them to provide a protective grid in your home. You would do this by putting Selenite or Black Tourmaline in each corner of your room or home.

- You can use them in energy healing practices to amplify, clear, or balance energy. I will set crystals on people as I'm doing Reiki energy healing.

There are also crystal beds that are created for the purpose of energy healing.

- You may use crystals with the intention of balancing your chakras. You can set the appropriate crystal on each chakra point while laying down and visualizing each chakra color as a spinning ball of light at that point. Or if you are focusing on a particular chakra, you can hold the crystal in your hand, while focusing on your intention and that specific chakra that may need some energy work.

- You can create crystal elixirs by placing crystals in your drinking water. The energetic vibration from the crystals has a positive effect on the water. The energy you send out through your thoughts and emotions also has an effect on water. You can not only use crystals, but with your intention send a blessing for the water, and also there are stickers with positive words that you can put on a water jar as well. It really makes a difference. Take into consideration that our bodies are approximately 70% water. Shungite will also purify water. When creating gem elixirs, only use sufficiently hard, non-water soluble, non-toxic stones. You do not want to use crystals that will dissolve in water, such as Selenite or Himalayan Salt. You also want to avoid toxic stones, such as Malachite, Pyrite, Galena, Cinnabar, Azurite, among others.

- Selenite is excellent for clearing energy. I use it in the clearing sprays we offer in the store, along with other crystals mixed in depending on the specific intention. We also use it in our bath salts and body scrubs.

- I've heard some people taking their crystals in the bath with them to absorb the higher vibrational energy.

- Some people use crystal spheres or flat surfaces for scrying, to receive psychic information.

- You may use oils that have been infused with the energy from crystals. These oils can be used for chakra balancing or we use some before meditations and distance healing sessions. You can use them at the 3rd eye chakra, or you can put some on your hands and breathe it in, or on pulse points.

- You may also create a crystal grid that uses multiple crystals working together for a specific intention.

People always ask if the size and shape of the crystal makes a difference. It does for the amount and the flow of the energy. The larger the crystal, the more surface space for energy to flow from, so a larger crystal will give off more energy than a small crystal. That doesn't mean that a small crystal isn't as effective, especially since it is easier to hold or have a smaller crystal with you, where the larger size crystal would most likely stay put, and provide positive energy for a space.

The shape of the crystal will also affect the flow of energy. For example, a pyramid shape will always have the majority of the energy flowing through the top point. Spheres will give off energy equally in all directions. If the crystals come to a point, then the energy would flow through the point. If it is double terminated, it has points on both sides, and the energy would flow out from both directions.

Crystals do absorb energy and may need to be cleansed occasionally. Cleansing is a way of re-tuning the energies of the crystal back to their original energetic frequency. Think of it like a guitar; when it has been moved around or frequently played the sound might need to be re-tuned to bring it back to its perfect sound. The same goes for re-tuning (cleansing) the energies of the crystal. There are many ways to cleanse a crystal.

- Selenite is excellent for clearing energy, and it will clear all of your other crystals. You can lay the crystal on a flat piece of Selenite, and that is all that would need to be done.

- You can put the crystals out in the sunlight or in a windowpane where they will receive sun. Be careful though, as some crystals, such as Amethyst, Rose Quartz, Smokey Quartz, Citrine, and Celestite will fade in the sun.

- Putting crystals in the moonlight will also cleanse them, and this is safe for all crystals. The full moon is a great time to cleanse and charge your crystals.

- You can also clear your crystals with your intention of sending out clearing energy from your hands and holding them over the crystals.

- You can put the crystals under running water, with the intention of having the water clear the energy. This method should not be done on all crystals, as some crystals such as Hematite, Magnetite, and Lodestone will oxidize if left under water too long. Also, crystals like Selenite, Himalayan Salt, and Halite will dissolve in water.

- You can place them in a bowl of rice or salt to clear them as well. Salt can potentially damage the surface of softer crystals.

- The Earth will also cleanse the energies of crystals. You can bury the crystals in the ground or in a pot of soil.

- You may also cleanse crystals with Sage or Palo Santo, the same as you would use to clear the energy in your home. Incense will work in a similar way to cleanse the energy, although it is not as powerful.

- Sound vibrations will also clear crystals. Crystal or Tibetan singing bowls work perfectly. Have your crystals near the bowl as you play it. You can run a tuning fork over your crystals, use a bell, tingshas (Tibetan cymbals), or drums. Any loud music will work as well. Put your crystals in front of the speakers and turn up your favorite music. The important thing with sound cleansing is to have the crystals within the sound's vibrations.

- There are some crystals that are self-cleansing, such as Selenite and Kyanite. There are others that some suggest that don't need cleansing, but those are the only two that I feel that are completely self-cleansing.

You will also hear people refer to charging crystals, but through the process of cleaning or clearing, you are also charging the crystal. In other words, you are removing all the lower vibrational energy, which brings the crystal back to its original and highest vibrational state.

Crystals also hold information and our intentions as well. You can hold the crystal with the intention of programing it with what you want to achieve from it. Programming is you putting your intentions of how you would like to work with the crystal within the crystal and also out into the Universe. Essentially you are infusing your desires with the crystal. You are inspiring it through your intention to help you attract and amplify those prayers that you are sending out into the Universe.

212

Think about your purpose for the stone while holding it, or holding your hands over the crystal. Visualize what it would be like to have your desire fulfilled. Feel what it will feel like, once you attract what you want into your life. Focus on the result that you would like to achieve, not what is lacking, as what you focus on and send out in the form of energy is what you attract back into your reality. Visualize and feel energy coming from the highest point in the Universe, down through the top of your head, down to your heart center, and down your arms, and through your hands to the crystal while focusing on your intention.

This is working to program the crystal with your intention, and it will also work through the energy that you are sending out into the universal energy field to attract back what is matching to the energetic vibration. Every time you look at the crystal, you will be reminded of your intention, and that will affect the energy you are sending out to the Universe. You will be receiving benefits both from the energy of the crystal and from the law of attraction.

You can also use crystals together in a grid for a specific intention. A crystal grid is a special grouping of stones laid out in a particular formation for a specific purpose. When created and empowered with intention, each stone within the grid amplifies the qualities and energy of the other stones. Lines of high frequency light link the stones and create a vortex of energy.

- The first step in creating a crystal grid would be to determine what your intention is. You may want to manifest abundance, love, protection, spiritual connection, or tranquility as some examples.

- Then you would want to decide on what crystals to use for the grid, based on what you are trying to achieve. Use what you know about the properties of the crystals as well as your intuition when selecting your crystals.

- Select a crystal amplifier for your center piece of the grid. I would usually use a clear crystal point that will stand upright.

- Make sure to cleanse and program each of the crystals to be used.

- You can write your intention down on a piece of paper and put it underneath your crystal grid or under the center crystal.

- Symbols and colors also have their own vibration. Decide on if you want to use a mandala to place your crystals on, and if so, which one will help amplify your intentions. You may also want to add color to your mandala or symbol to help with the energies created with your crystal grid.

- You may want to add a candle as well, as they also work with your intention.

- Even though you programmed each crystal, once the crystal grid is completed, you can set your intention and program your grid as a whole, in the same way.

BRING WHAT YOU DESIRE INTO YOUR REALITY

Once you have created what you wanted, know that you have the power to consciously create all that you desire in life. There is power in looking back and knowing that you have succeeded every time that you have used the information you learned about in this book to manifest what you wanted. This confidence will help you as you move forward with creating all you want in life. It is an ongoing journey, and you will be inspired and guided through your intuition to create more and more wonderful things that will bring you the highest level of wellbeing in all areas of your life. You are in control of it all.

MANIFEST THROUGH THE CHAKRAS

You can also look at manifesting as moving through the chakras. Usually when we work through the chakras, we start at the bottom (root chakra), which is more closely related to the physical world, and work our way up to the highest chakra (crown chakra), which is related to the higher dimensions of consciousness. When looking at manifestation, we start at the top and work our way down, because we are working with higher dimensional energies, and bringing what we want into our reality in the physical world.

Crown Chakra-
This is your consciousness and your connection to the field. It is what starts the creation process.

Third Eye Chakra-
Listening and trusting your intuition, which is going to guide you to what you want to manifest and the knowing of how to move forward.

Throat Chakra-
This is about being able to express and communicate what it is you want to manifest. You need to have the clarity in order to be able to express it. This would include writing or speaking your intentions as well as working with others, including higher dimensional energies.

Heart Chakra-
Listening to your heart and coming from a place of love.

Solar Plexus Chakra-
Having the confidence to take inspired action.

Sacral Chakra-
Feeling the passion and emotion of what you want to manifest.

Root chakra-
Bringing and experiencing what you created into your physical reality.

There are no limitations on what you can create, as long as you truly believe that you can, you are able to focus and master your thoughts, emotions, and intentions, and then listen to your intuition and take inspired action to lead you to what you wanted to create. Anything is possible!

You are creating your reality, whether you are doing it consciously or not. It is up to you whether you choose to react to what you are currently experiencing or to consciously create everything you desire to experience in your life.

Know your power!

SUMMARY OF KEY #3: CONSCIOUSLY CREATING ALL YOU DESIRE

- Your energetic vibration affects your ability to manifest as well as how quickly you can bring what you desire into your life. The higher your vibration the easier it is to consciously create the experiences you prefer in your life.

- You are not manifesting anything out of nothing. Everything already exists. If you can think it, it is already there in the field as a potential that is available to be tapped into with a matching vibration.

- You are creating your reality, whether you realize it or not. It is either done in chaos based on reaction to what you are currently experiencing or done consciously to create what you prefer to experience.

- What you are currently experiencing was created from old energy, past thoughts and beliefs. To create something different for the future, then you need to change your way of thinking in the present.

- It is important to take the time to think about what you would like to bring into your life. If you get too focused on what already is part of your reality with work, chores, bills, and all of the other day to day activities of life, then you are not opening yourself up to all of the wonderful potentials that are available for you to bring into your life.

- There are no limitations on what you can create. Anything is possible as long as you truly believe that you can, and you are able to focus and master your thoughts, emotions, and intentions, and listen to your intuition and take inspired action to lead you to what you want to create.

- It is important to know your power as a multi-dimensional being and to know that you are in control of what you experience in life.

- It is also important to understand and utilize the law of attraction, knowing that you experience what you are a vibrational match to. Everything that you experience is a reflection of your state of being and what you are tapping into energetically though your consciousness.

- The law of cause and effect determines that nothing that happens is random. There is a cause for every effect, and visa versa. Every thought, emotion, and action will create a vibration that will be reflected back to you in your life. What you send out energetically is what you will receive back.

- Make sure that what you desire is in alignment with your soul self, and not just your ego or logical mind.

- Be guided by the higher dimensional part of yourself, and not by other people's expectations or guidance.

- Listen to your intuition. This is how your higher self communicates to you and helps to lead you to the highest potential available.

- Come from a place of love in the manifestation process. If you are creating out of fear of what you do not want to experience, that will cause resistance.

- Trust is a powerful force that will allow the creation process to move forward without adding the resistance of uncertainty.

- It is important to be clear about what you want to create in your experience, but don't be insistent that it has to be that exact manifestation, or you won't be happy. Be open to go with the flow of what your higher self is guiding you to, as it may be even better than your logical mind could have imagined.

- It is important to focus on what you desire, and not how to get it. Allow your higher self to find the path of least resistance.

- In any situation, if you follow the option that brings you the strongest feeling of joy or excitement, without fear, you will be headed towards the path for your highest good. You can use that feeling as a guidance system.

- The feelings of joy, peace, and unconditional love are your true nature. It is only beliefs and thoughts that create resistance and hold you back from experiencing your true self. You can use them as an indication of something being out of alignment with your higher self, and then you can shift your thoughts to remove all resistance to your highest state of wellbeing and manifestation.

- Feel the emotion of what you want to manifest as if it has already happened. It is that emotion that will help you to match that vibration of what you want to experience.

- Visualization is a powerful tool. Once you have used the images to experience the emotion of what you want to create, then release them with the intention of being open to something even better.

- Communication of what you want to bring into your experience is also helpful. It helps bring the energy into your physical reality. You can communicate with someone who can help you in the manifestation or to higher vibrational energies that can help guide you to what you prefer.

- Feel gratitude for everything wonderful in your life and everything wonderful that is yet to come. The vibration of gratitude helps create more experiences to be grateful for.

- Make sure that there are not any limiting beliefs or thoughts that are holding you back from anything you desire. If there are, then let them go and align yourself with beliefs and thoughts that would help you to experience everything you desire.

- Prayer and meditation are also tools to help you in the manifestation process. Prayer is communicating to higher dimensional energies. Meditation is quieting the mind to listen and also to release the resistance of lower vibrational thoughts.

- Because we live in the physical world, it will usually be necessary to take inspired action to bring what you desire into your life. Your higher self will guide you to the steps to take through your intuition, synchronicity, and the feeling of joy.

- Look at challenges as an opportunity to find solutions. The solution will never come from focusing on the problems.

- Affirmations are very powerful tools, especially when they start with "I am". Be very careful with your wording and vibrational state. If you are in the state of "wanting" that is a different vibration than that of "experiencing" or "having". If it is something that you "will do", that is also a different vibration than that of "doing".

- Water crystals are affected by vibration as well and the water will hold intention. You can put your intention into the water you drink, the food you eat, or the air you breathe.

- Divination tools such as muscle testing, the pendulum, Tarot or oracle cards, or message boards can help bring guidance from your higher self to assist in the manifestation process.

- Other tools that can be utilized in manifesting are crystals, candles, and oils. Vision boards can also be helpful reminders of your intentions.

- You can also utilize the chakras as a tool of realization of the manifesting process.

IN CONCLUSION

Anyone can utilize the information in this book and consciously create everything they desire in life! There isn't anything difficult about it, but it does take some awareness and a willingness to change the way you think about yourself and your life. It is important to do the introspective work to be aware of what your beliefs, thoughts, and emotions are and be willing to shift them to be in alignment with everything in life you desire.

You are creating your reality, and it is up to you to choose whether to consciously create the life of your dreams or to create out of the chaos of random thoughts and emotions that are reactions to what you are experiencing in this illusion that we call life.

Everything is energy! That is all there is to it. It is all vibration. Your life is a reflection of your consciousness. What you desire already exists, and you just need to be a vibrational match in order to see it. When you have a true understanding of this, then you can let go of all resistance of lower vibrational beliefs and thoughts and raise your vibration so that you are in alignment with your higher self. Then you can choose your thoughts that create the emotions that match to the vibration of what you want to experience in life.

Allow your higher self to guide you through intuition, joy, and synchronicity to take inspired action where needed. Then allow everything you desire into your experience. There are no limitations, other than your own mind, and you can be in control of that, if you choose to be. Master the mind and become the master of creating your reality in the way that you desire.

Utilize the keys to creation to consciously create all you desire in life. These are the keys to creation.

1) Understand how the Universe works and who you are as a multi-dimensional being.

2) Know the importance of your energetic vibration and raise it to be more in alignment with your higher self.

3) Tap into what already exists as electromagnetic potentials within the quantum field of "All That Is" and allow what you desire into the experience of your physical reality.

That really is all there is to it. This is not new age philosophy. This is how the Universe works. What is considered as spiritual or metaphysical is just physics that is not yet understood by humanity.

You experience what is a vibrational match. What you give is what you receive back. It is not possible for any other result, so make sure that you are giving energetically, though your thoughts and emotions, what you want to have reflected back into your life.

You are so much more than your physical experience of life. You are a higher dimensional being that is using a very small amount of that energy of who you really are to experience the process of creation, though the illusion of time and space, in order to be able to experience what already is from a different perspective. That is how growth and expansion happen at a soul level.

You are a part of the creative source, All That Is, or what some would call God. Know your power! Don't limit yourself. You are a powerful creator!

If you choose to utilize all of the information you learned in this book, you will consciously create the life of your dreams. You will be able to experience all you desire in your life!

ABOUT THE AUTHOR

Michelle Orlijan is a spiritual medium, a healer, teacher, and an author. She and her husband own a beautiful metaphysical store and healing studio in Riverside, CA called "The Sacred Journey", and the website is: www.sacredjourneyshop.com. Her other books include "Working with Energy", "Communicating with Spirit", and "The Tarot Guide".

Made in the USA
Middletown, DE
11 March 2022

62349049R00136